BrokerVision

Practical Wisdom for Real Estate Agents

Jason Crouch

Pamela Crouch &
Aleah Crouch, Editors

For my family
I love you all so much

Copyright © 2020 Jason Crouch
First Edition
ISBN 978-1-7355307-1-0
Cover Image by Gilbert Sauceda

Contents

Introduction: Who Am I? 7

Chapter 1: Getting Started 11
My Favorite Part of Real Estate...11
Is Real Estate Right for You? 12
    Likeability 13
    Intelligence...14
    Trustworthiness/honesty 14
    Service mentality 14
    Friendliness...14
    Sense of humor...14
    Confidence 15
    Work ethic...15
    Sphere of influence 15
    Listening and communication skills 16
    Thick skin..16
Landing Your First Client 16
Perception is Everything 20
"Who Will Work with Me?" 21
Feeling Uncomfortable Is Expected 24

Chapter 2: Marketing..27
Ask for the Business! What Do You Have to Lose? 27
Consistent Marketing Will Equal Results 29
How Much Should You Focus Your Marketing?...........................30
Networking—How to Be the Most Popular Person in the Room..31

Chapter 3: Working with Buyers 33
How to Present and Use Buyer Representation Agreements 37
Showing Properties to the Client..38
    Set the tone at the outset..38

    Spend time preparing 38
    Be honest 40
    Note taking 41
    Know your goal when you start the day 41
    Chatting all day 41
The Inspection 44
After the Inspection: Negotiating Repairs 44
Closing Day 45
Working with a New Home Buyer 46
Helping Choosy Buyers "Pull the Trigger" with a Contract 51
Making Things Right 53
Active Listening 56
"Should We State a Deadline to Respond to Our Offer?" 57
Additional Tips for Buyer's Agents 58

Chapter 4: Working with Sellers 61

Quick Steps to Doing a CMA (Comparative Market Analysis) for a Home 61
You're Going to a Listing Appointment? How to Win Almost Every Time 64
Using Your Powers of Observation to List More Homes 66
Multiple Offers 70
Contract to Closing Process as a Listing Agent 72
Inspection Repair Request 72
Moving Toward Closing 73
Smell Your Way to Success 74
Top 7 Common Mistakes to Avoid When Listing a Home 75
    Overpricing 76
    Neglecting Necessary Repairs 76
    Neglecting to Stage the Home 77
    Allowing Sellers to Get Hung Up on Small Stuff 77
    Allowing Emotional Issues to Dictate the Transaction 78
    Selling at the Wrong Time 78
    Not Giving Potential Buyers Access to the Home 79
What Does "Value" Mean? 79
"Bring All Offers" and "Price Firm" are Not Synonymous! 81

Chapter 5: General Advice for All Agents 83
Setting Expectations with Clients 83
How to Avoid Getting Sued — My Humble Opinion 84
"Are You Already Working with an Agent?" 87
How to Guide Clients Through the Real Estate Maze....................88
Some Unique Tips for Communicating with Clients......................91
Dealing with Conflict During Transactions 93
The Only Thing that Stays Constant Is Change..............................94
The Secret Ingredient Is Empathy 95
Dealing with Unprofessional Advisers..97
"I Hate to Be the Bearer of Bad News, But...." 99
What You Can Control 100

Chapter 6: Working with Related Industries..............103
You Can Do Everything Right and Still Not Get Paid..................103
Who's on Your Team?...104
Selecting the Right Supporting Cast 105
Choosing Good Loan Officers...106
Recommending Inspectors 108
Recommending Title and Escrow Services 109
The Importance of Appraisals...110

Chapter 7: Negotiating 113
There Is a Difference between Bluffing and Good Negotiating ..113
Negotiating 101 — You Can't Manufacture Leverage 114
Commission Issues 117

Chapter 8: Things That Go Broke in the Night: Real Estate Horror Stories 119

Chapter 9: Other Assorted Bonus Advice 127
Industry Myth—"Real Estate Agents and Brokers Are Greedy" 127
Are Real Estate Clients Brand Loyal or Agent Loyal? 128
Handling Tough Situations Gracefully 130
Patience Pays Off...132
Magic Words..133
"You Really Should Have Pushed Me Harder!" 134

Chapter 10: Conclusion 137

Index 139

Introduction: Who Am I?

Hey there — First of all, welcome to my mind. If you bought this book, you might want to learn a little more about me.

If not, that's okay, too.

If so, here's some basic info:

I was born and raised in Dallas, Texas. I have lived in Texas my entire life. I love it here. I moved to the Austin area (Georgetown) in 1988 to attend Southwestern University, which is my alma mater. I have a bachelor's degree in business administration with a minor in economics.

I met my awesome wife Pam in 1991 on the dance floor of an Austin nightclub. We married a couple of years later. We have four kids, currently ages 21, 19, 14, and 11. Our son is the oldest, and we have three daughters.

After college, I worked a few jobs in retail and restaurant management before starting my own small business with a friend. We provided real estate photography and printing services, and then we decided to get licensed around the beginning of 1997. I have been in full-time real estate sales since then.

In the fall of 2004, I founded my own real estate brokerage, Austin Texas Homes, along with my business partners. I serve as the broker and I am one of the owners. We manage a terrific, ethical, smart group of agents who handle residential and commercial real estate sales and leasing throughout the Austin/Central Texas area.

While I do have experience with several other areas of real estate, this book is intended to help you primarily with residential sales, representing clients who are buying or selling a primary residence.

I've personally sold and helped to manage home sales totaling hundreds of millions of dollars, and I have trained dozens of agents over the years, some of whom are now successful brokers with their own companies. I have also served as a paid coach in other markets around the country.

On a personal note, I am a Christian, and I am an ordained deacon in the Presbyterian Church in America (PCA). We helped to plant our church (Christ Presbyterian Church) in 2008 in Georgetown.

In 2014, I was pleasantly surprised to receive the "Texas Realtor Hero" award from the Texas Association of Realtors based on the ministry that I founded with my wife to help homeless and needy families. A few months later, I also received the Community Service Award from the Austin Board of Realtors.

Generally speaking, I love what I get to do for a living. I have been blessed in so many ways in this industry. There have been some difficult days, and some stressful times, but I'm happy and content overall.

I genuinely hope you find value in this book. It's been a long-time goal of mine to be an author. I have enjoyed writing and reading for as long as I can remember.

This book is intended to be valuable for both new and experienced agents, though many of the lessons in the early chapters will be more helpful for newer agents.

Please bear in mind that all my real estate sales experience is in the state of Texas. While some of the advice I give in this book is applicable anywhere, some of it is also specific to Texas. As a general word of advice, it's best to seek answers from your broker. If you don't have a broker who is available to answer questions, you should consider getting a better one. If you're local, call me and let's talk.

I feel certain that no matter how long I spend revising this before I decide to publish it, I will probably still forget to include some important points. If you have questions, feel free to reach out to me via email or on my phone, which is always nearby.

Mostly, I want to thank you for taking the time to read this book. It means a lot to me, I assure you. I hope you find it to be a helpful resource.

Jason Crouch
jcrouchbroker@gmail.com
(512) 796-7653 (cell)
October 16, 2020

Chapter 1

Getting Started

Let's jump right in, shall we? Before you embark on a career in real estate, I recommend evaluating your personal skill set. You should also consider where your initial clients will come from, and how you will continue to get business over time.

In my opinion, there are no "regular" jobs that can prepare you for the world of straight commission real estate sales work. This work can be grueling, difficult, and frustrating, but it can also be incredibly rewarding, fulfilling, and lucrative.

In the sections ahead, I will cover many of the basics about getting up and running. I hope you find this both helpful and encouraging.

My Favorite Part of Real Estate

I occasionally get asked the question above. I've thought about this a good deal over the years.

My absolute favorite part is too easy to guess—getting paid. (Thanks, Captain Obvious.) Beyond that, the answer comes in two parts.

First, I have a higher-level view: As a career, I most enjoy the fact that I get to meet so many different people of all backgrounds and interests, and I'm able to see a variety of properties, so every day is different. This is fun for me. Some people thrive on routine and predictability. I do not. I enjoy exploring and learning new things and getting to know my clients.

Second, regarding the day-to-day work of selling, I most enjoy seeing that moment when one of my clients decides on the right home for their various needs and wants, no matter what the price range is. I've seen that twinkle in my clients' eyes hundreds of times, but I never get tired of it. This could be a Lake Austin waterfront estate, or a downtown condo, or a simple two-bedroom home in a modest neighborhood—when a client finds the right home, I get a little rush of adrenaline every single time. It shows me that I'm doing my job correctly. I've provided good service, and I've managed to help someone find the perfect place for *them*.

It means I listened.

Also, and this only came to me as I was typing, this feeling of business competence ("I'm actually doing this") is likely rooted in my own childhood, when I just sort of knew I wanted to have my own business. Back then, I wanted to be one of two things: a comedian, or a pediatrician.

I still love to make people laugh, but most of my real-life medical experience has come from helping my own kids with Band-Aids and comforting them when they get hurt, and I'm completely happy with that. I really do love my life.

But let's get back to my favorite part of selling homes.

"Jason, this is the one. Let's make an offer."

This is absolute music to my ears. And on a deeper level, it gives me a sense of satisfaction, not just because I will make money, but because I'm helping someone to decide on their new home. It's hard to think of a more personal large purchase or decision than that.

I am thankful every day that I get to wake up and do this.

With that in mind….

Is Real Estate Right for You?

If you're still considering whether you should start a real estate career, you should take the time to read this section. If you're already licensed and looking for tips, feel free to skip ahead. If you're like me, you will probably still read this part no matter what.

At any rate, let's continue. Consider this section to be the view from the broker's desk, as someone who has witnessed many fledgling careers, some of which have blossomed, while others never seemed to get out of the starting gate at all. .

There are some agents who set solid high-income goals and work hard to attain them every year, while others do little planning and simply depend on referral business. Some consider themselves successful if they can replace their income from their previous career. Others mainly desire flexible hours for their work. No matter what your personality type is, you can probably succeed in real estate, although I recognize that each person's definition of "success" is uniquely personal.

A quick note about flexible hours: Licensed agents are almost always self-employed independent contractors, so being your own boss certainly allows you to set your own schedule. This is liberating if you've been an employee for years, but it's also challenging because you need to find ways to market yourself if you want to make money selling homes.

I have hired and trained dozens of agents during my own career with the company that I own and operate, and I have noticed some common traits that successful agents share.

I will admit that I am still sometimes surprised by which ones "make it" and which ones simply don't, though these surprises are less frequent now.

Here are some characteristics that help:

Likeability

When I am interviewing a potential agent, there are a few things that go through my mind, but the first (and perhaps the most obvious) thing I ask myself is: "Do I like this person?"

I don't mean "Can we be best friends?", but is this person inherently likeable? If not, why continue any further?

Having said that, I have encountered plenty of seemingly successful agents over the years who are not pleasant or even particularly nice or decent. In their case, I think they may have clients who appreciate the perception that their chosen agent is a no-nonsense "bulldog" who will fight for them, which could be true. It's just not the way I do things. I think it's important to push hard for our clients, but it's also important to remain respectful.

Intelligence

This is important. For those of us who have been in this industry for years, we've all had experiences with "that moron" handling the other side of the deal.

As a broker, I have enough potential liabilities lurking out there already without taking a risk on hiring someone who is clearly dull. However, one of the reasons I started working on getting my real estate license in 1996 was the fact that I knew so many agents making good money who weren't exactly rocket scientists. The pre-licensing educational bar has been raised since then, and I've heard that the licensing test is quite a bit harder these days, which is a good thing for our industry.

Trustworthiness/honesty

In order to gain clients and sell real estate, you need a network of people who both know you and trust you. Integrity is something that seems to be in shorter supply these days, so an honest agent will be able to reap the benefits of a foundation of happy clients.

Service mentality

Do you like helping people? I have met thousands of agents over the course of my career. The best ones have a sincere desire to provide top-notch service in a spirit of giving. Also, as Realtors, we are supposed to place the needs of our clients above our own interests.

Friendliness

Are you a good conversationalist? Do you genuinely enjoy meeting people from all backgrounds and learning about them? At its core, real estate is a relationship business. For years, I have considered myself to be in the friend-making business. I heard this somewhere from a real estate coach, and it stuck with me. .

Sense of humor

There are countless times in my own career that I was able to defuse a potentially volatile situation with a dose of humor. It also helps when you're grieving the loss of a sale.

Confidence

Simply put, if you are not comfortable in your own skin, chances are that you will not succeed in real estate. When you're starting out, you need to have confidence in your broker or mentor at an absolute minimum, so that you know you can quickly get answers to questions you may not be able to easily answer yet.

When it comes to real estate sales, you are the product. This is a competitive business, and people can easily find another agent to help them acquire a property, so you need to be confident that you are the best possible choice for your clients.

A straight-commission sales career is not for the weak. It takes a measure of bravery to know that you will not have income unless you sell something. Beyond that, you need to be brave enough to talk to some strangers on the phone or meet them in person sometimes. Confidence is required when it is time to look someone in the eye and tell them that you are the best agent for them.

Work ethic

Do you have the ability and desire to work hard? I don't necessarily mean long, grueling hours. I'm talking about the basics of real estate for as far back as any of us can remember: developing relationships, responding to phone calls, texts, and random emails, "closing" someone on a transaction, being available at odd hours to answer questions, etc. Yes, you can set your own hours, but when there is the siren call of a large commission, you'll want to be available to make it happen.

Sphere of influence

This refers to the number of people you know. Maybe stated more clearly, it's the people who know you.

Perhaps you know everyone at church, or you coach a team for your kids. Maybe you've lived in the area a long time and you were in sales in a different field. Maybe you used to work as a school principal or teacher, and you know tons of families in the area already. Maybe you taught Sunday school, or you organized a club for homeschoolers.

All of these are valuable networks.

I have come to value the ability to network over many other typical "sales" skills now. A larger group of people to draw from means more potential opportunities to help them when the time is right to buy or sell a home.

Listening and communication skills

Some people assume that being successful in sales mainly means being a good talker. There is some truth in this, but I've found it's infinitely more important to be a good listener, and to be able to communicate effectively in writing. I can't count the number of times that I was able to salvage a deal because I was able to convey things directly and concisely in writing. When you can listen well, you will be in tune with your clients, which will help you to react as needed and to better assist them.

Thick skin

This seems to help, especially early on, when you will almost certainly experience rejection from clients and even from friends. Real estate is probably not the right business for someone who is overly sensitive to rejection. Frankly, I am rather sensitive myself, but time and trials have forced me to learn not to take things too personally. I'm still working on this.

I hope you find this list helpful. It is not exhaustive, of course, but it's a great starting point.

Speaking of starting points, if you have already decided to get your license, here are some great basic tips on how to start making money…

LANDING YOUR FIRST CLIENT

Some of the information below may seem rudimentary or even "old school," but the fundamentals of real estate have never changed much.

You will probably hear this next sentence countless times as you embark on a sales career, and you may already know it:

> ***Your ability to succeed in real estate is based on the number of people who know you, like you, and trust you.***

Know, like, and trust. This seems simple enough, right?

I heard a powerful addition to this old mantra from a real estate marketing guru once. He said our success is determined by those who know you, like you, trust you, and *remember* you.

That last element is important. Timing is everything in this business. You can work with a buyer who is loyal and content with your services, then lose touch with him/her for a month and discover that they wandered into a builder's model and bought a home without you.

If you connect with your friends and acquaintances via social media (and I highly recommend this, because you can do it for free), it's easier than ever to stay in touch with current and past clients.

When you launch your real estate business, hope and optimism spring eternal. It seems like easy money … until you try to land a buyer or seller and get them all the way to the closing table.

Like the great Paul Simon song "50 Ways to Leave Your Lover," there are countless ways to lose a buyer. Maybe their financing doesn't work out because the lender wasn't thorough enough. Maybe the buyer just gets cold feet and flakes out for no readily apparent reason. Just know that this type of thing WILL happen. Don't let it stop you.

People will disappoint you. Keep going.

Here are some steps you can take right away:

1. Make a list of *everyone* you know, even if you don't know them well. Use your phone contacts, Facebook friend list, etc. Do not limit this list to those who are local. Consider every single person whom you know to be part of your sphere of influence. Some are stronger additions, of course, but you may be surprised by which casual acquaintances will send you business.

2. Make it clear to everyone on the above list that you are in real estate. I will leave it up to you to determine which method best suits you (letters, posts on social media, phone calls, texts— you make this decision). Which one works best? The answer is: whichever one you will actually do. A combination of different types of contact methods is good to try.

3. Demonstrate that you enjoy what you're doing now. This is not hard, I promise. Just say it. "I love selling homes" or "I love

helping my clients get top dollar for their homes," etc. As you may recall from the last chapter (if you read it), this business is not rocket science.

4. Ask for the business. This sounds easy on the surface while you are sitting in a coffee shop or reading, but it's a little more daunting when you are out and about and face to face with your friends and other potential clients. You must tell people that you want to help. Just say, "I really want to be your Realtor" and if they are not ready to do anything currently, tell them you want to help when the time is right.

Make it a goal to tell everyone you meet three things:

- You are in real estate
- You love what you do (assuming it's the truth), and ...
- You want to help them.

If you can do these three things consistently, it will pay off.

When you are starting out, get business cards and give them out like you have a time limit, because you might. Typically, it takes several months to start making money selling houses. The only way to accelerate this process is to get more opportunities more quickly. That means you can't be shy about promoting your business. As I said above, you are the product you're selling. You may be feeling that you can't truly add value yet, but once you are licensed, you will already know more about real estate than most of your potential clients.

I recommend getting a name tag and wearing it everywhere. It's imperative that you get out of your house or office on a regular basis and spend time around people face-to-face. Beyond that, make a point to get your name out there on Facebook, Instagram, Twitter, LinkedIn, and anywhere else you have an account.

One other suggestion to get in front of more potential clients is to offer to teach a class on home buying (you may want to plan this with your broker to get an outline together). You can partner with a loan officer and get buyers pre-qualified while you are there together. They'll usually also split the tab for the venue or refreshments if it's an "in person" class, though you could also offer it online.

Sometimes, the best approach to landing your first client is simple honesty. Write a post on your platform of choice and ask your friends to keep you in mind as a resource for real estate.

One of the best and simplest techniques I have seen came from Brian Buffini, an international real estate coach. He calls this technique the "Mayor Campaign."

It goes like this: "Oh, by the way, if you were buying or selling a home, or had a friend or family member who was, do you have an agent you would refer them to?"

Or, for people you already know well: "Oh, by the way, if you were buying or selling a home, or had a friend or family member who was, am I the person you would refer them to?"

This question can help you to quickly determine if the person you're asking is a valid future referral source and/or prospect.

If they say that they do have someone in mind other than you, simply respond that you're happy that they have a resource already. (You may want to add that you hope they'll keep you in mind if things change—that is my only addition to Buffini's script).

If they say that they don't have anyone yet, respond with this:

"Well, I'd like to be that person … and from time to time I come across valuable real estate information that everyone finds helpful. Would you like to receive that?" If so, ask them where they would like to receive it, and add them to your database, and make a point to stay in touch.

If you can follow a decent percentage of the steps I have outlined above and use the Mayor Campaign to qualify and gain prospects, you will be well on your way.

Talk to everyone. Tell them what you do. Tell them how much you love it (if true). Mention that you want to help them. Ask the Mayor questions. It really is that simple, but it isn't always easy.

Beyond these ideas, you can find a ton of free real estate marketing content on YouTube and on podcasts like Pat Hiban's Real Estate Rockstars. At our company, we have always provided free training, but some brokerages do not, so I would encourage you to choose wisely. You want to work at a company with people who are supportive and helpful and who are genuinely invested in your success as a person.

I can assure you without hesitation that most agents do not effectively do the things I have discussed in this chapter. Truthfully, I do a middling job myself when it comes to prospecting for new business, but I have been around this business for a long time, so I am now working (almost) exclusively by referral and with past clients.

If you can form the right habits as you embark on this new venture, and if you can maintain enthusiasm over time, your business should begin to grow and flourish.

Perception is Everything

To enhance some of the suggestions from the previous chapter, I think it's worth discussing how you can become a trusted resource within your sphere of influence.

First, what is a "sphere of influence?" I like this simple definition I found on Contactually: Your sphere consists of "the folks in your network with whom your opinion holds some weight."

So how do you convince people that your opinion is worthwhile?

When you're a fledgling agent, this is a bit harder to do, especially with close friends who can see that you're just getting started. Ironically, friends are often harder to persuade than random strangers who have no history with you.

One of the best ways I have seen to demonstrate your ability early in your career is to give the perception that you are busy. Please note I'm *not* advocating being dishonest in any way. Instead, I recommend documenting your real estate activity publicly via social media or just talking about what you're working on at any given time. Here are some suggestions to consider:

- Videos of model homes
- Video interviews with local business owners
- Posts about open houses you are hosting
- Posts about other listings within your company (double check with your broker — we allow this for any of our listings)

- Talk about something you learned or an interesting class or online seminar you attended
- Mention it whenever you get a contract in place, or when you submit an offer ("Excited for my clients in (Mytown)! We just wrote an offer on their potential dream home.")

The bottom line here is that you can swiftly give the impression to friends and acquaintances that you're highly active in the real estate market.

Some of the most successful agents I have mentored over the years have used this technique. It should begin to enhance your reputation within your personal community.

Once you have built this foundation, the perception could begin to become a reality.

"Who Will Work with Me?"

This question is something that new agents should be focused on early, and this will always be an important facet of your business.

The quick answer is that pretty much everyone has the potential to work with you or to send you business, even if they don't live in your local market.

You will occasionally hear someone say that they don't choose to work with agents who are friends, because they don't want to ruin the friendship. I disagree with this perspective, partly because I always prefer to work with friends when I am choosing a service provider, and partly because I know that a friend will always care more about the outcome and take better care of me than someone I barely know.

Here's a sample "script" to help you handle this objection. Let's assume you already know that your friend Dave is looking to move.

YOU: Hey Dave, I heard you might be looking to move closer to town.

DAVE: Yeah, Nina and I were considering it. I'm tired of spending so much of my life in traffic.

YOU: I would love to help you with your home search. I can

help sell your current home, too.

DAVE: We were talking about it, and I don't want to use a friend because I'm worried that it might mess up the relationship if things don't go smoothly.

YOU: I can understand that, but from my own experience, the best person to help you is a friend, and I promise to take good care of you.

(If you're willing, you could also say, "I would be willing to charge you less to sell your home, especially if I can help with the purchase.")

If Dave seems indecisive, make sure to empathize and tell him that you understand he needs to include his wife in any decisions. This is something I have used that seems to help:

"I promise I understand the dynamic you're describing. Most of our transactions are smooth, and if problems arise, we make things right. Of all my clients, the overwhelming majority have given me positive feedback, and I know they would be happy to work with me again. If you give me a shot, I promise not to make you feel weird if it doesn't work out. Either way, I'm here if you need me."

This may seem a little wordy, and possibly a tad pushy, but it's also honest and direct and it addresses Dave's mental discomfort about the outcome of his sale and purchase.

Sometimes, people decide not to work with you. This is part of the gig, so it's best to just get accustomed to that notion early. Rejection is never easy, but some people are better at processing it quickly and moving on. I'm better at this than I used to be, but it still hurts sometimes.

Primarily, you need to keep your eyes open for opportunities and recognize that literally everyone you meet has the potential to help grow your business. This is not hyperbole. Some of my best clients have come from some surprising sources.

Here are some sources of business I have had personally, some of which are more traditional, and some of which may surprise you:

- Internet leads from our main website
- Blogging

- Magazine ads
- Targeted Facebook ads
- Church
- Referrals from agents in other cities
- Referrals from local agents who work other parts of town
- Networking events
- Speaking gig which came from blogging efforts
- Corporate relocation accounts (landed two of these by working with clients who appreciated our service)
- Referrals from past clients (this is the lifeblood of our business)
- Referrals from clients who were represented by another agent on a transaction I worked (there is a lesson therein)
- Family
- Friends of my family
- Neighbors (this should seem obvious, I suppose)
- Referral from an agent who was retiring
- Referrals from lenders
- My wife's book club
- Buyers from my listings who then list their homes with me
- A Facebook post with a list of questions I had answered for a potential client
- A letter written directly to a specific home that my friends were interested in
- Local radio DJ whom I marketed to a few times (several referrals plus his home sale)
- A broker friend of mine in another city sitting on a plane next to someone she later referred to me

Clearly, with any of these sources, there are branches and relationships which can lead to additional sales for you.

You get the picture. Don't limit yourself.

Unlike some products and businesses, most people are interested in the local real estate market, whether they are considering buying, considering selling, or even if they just want to know how their investment is faring. Maybe they just have a general level of interest. You can use this interest to talk about what you do with less fear of being "that guy" or "that lady" who is always hawking something.

Feeling Uncomfortable Is Expected

My wife and I have a long-standing joke about the popular 1960's show Gilligan's Island: "Hey, do you remember that episode of Gilligan's Island when it looked like they were about to get off the island, but then Gilligan made some ridiculous mistake and they had to stay there?"

If you have seen this show, then you know that almost *every* episode revolves around the premise in the question above. *Gilligan always managed to find a way to mess up their plans of being rescued.*

When I first started in real estate, I didn't have any listings, so I tried working with buyers that first year. I must admit, I felt like Gilligan. Every time I would get close to writing an offer or closing a sale, I would say or do something wrong or circumstances would just come together badly, and things would fall apart.

At one point, in late 1997, I distinctly remember questioning whether I wanted to work with buyers ever again, since they seemed disloyal, difficult, and disheartening (I wasn't trying to force the alliteration here, but it seems to work).

My broker at the time was a wise man, and he told me that in the first year, things are just harder to close. Some stray detail is overlooked, or clients can sense that you don't know real estate all that well yet, so they get a bit skittish.

Since about 1999 or 2000, I have closed more sales with buyers than with sellers, which would have seemed impossible to me back when I had those early self-doubts.

I also distinctly remember taking a walk around our neighborhood with my wife in 1998, when we were expecting our first child. I expressed to her that I wasn't sure if I should continue in real estate at all, considering our finances back then and the fact that it was so difficult to be self-employed with no regular income.

Her question to me that evening during our walk has resonated for over 20 years now, through good times and tough times.

"Well, can you think of anything else that you could do right now with a higher earning potential?"

"No, not really," I replied.

"Then I guess you need to keep doing it."

That was easy! You can see why I married her. I'm glad she's always been there to support me, and things (of course) improved for us financially. I was able to start my own brokerage firm here in Austin about six years after that evening conversation.

So, if you feel like Gilligan sometimes — maybe a little clumsy as you are starting out, finding your way and trying not to embarrass yourself with clients, just know that everyone starts somewhere, and most people have doubts along the way.

Chapter 2

Marketing

Marketing your services is an ongoing task, no matter how many years you have been in real estate. There are no hard-and-fast rules about which type of marketing is best, but if you want a consistent flow of business, you will have to get your name out there somehow.

Some people are born marketers, while others are intimidated by the concept. If it helps, just think of marketing in a simpler way: it's how you plan to tell people about your availability and desire to help with their needs.

ASK FOR THE BUSINESS! WHAT DO YOU HAVE TO LOSE?

Years ago, someone called me from the sign on one of my listings in north Austin, and we set up an appointment to look at the home that evening. He sounded like a nice young guy on the phone when we spoke, and we had a great instant rapport during the showing. I noticed that he was carrying a spiral notebook with notes about lots of other houses (along with agent names, phone numbers, etc.)

We spent a while looking around and talking about the area and the market in general, and he was hoping his wife could make it to see the place, too. I told him that I didn't have any other appointments that day for several hours, so I was available if we needed to wait on her to see it. This made him happy and he tried to call his wife a few times, to no avail.

I told him that I would be happy to help him if he was looking at a lot of homes in the area (I already knew he didn't have an agent). I also mentioned that I would be happy to come back if his wife were able to make it that day. He was noncommittal, but pleasant overall. I gave him my business card before he left.

Thankfully, I got a call from him about an hour later, asking if I could show him and his wife a couple of other homes in the neighborhood. It turned out that both homes were vacant, so I didn't even have to make any appointments.

I told him that I could easily meet with them, and he said, "That's great! I just want to get your opinion on those so that we can make a decision. I have narrowed it down to three homes, and we will be buying something soon. I'm going to go through you when I buy."

After showing him the other places, I didn't think my listing was the best fit for him, his wife, and their four-year-old son. I gave him my honest opinion about the pros and cons of each home, and he chose a different place. *The point here is that I gained a new buyer by simply being available and mentioning that I would like to help him.*

I realized that I might have been the first person to even ask for his business. I didn't pressure him at all. I just offered my services if he needed them. This has been my method for many years, but I wondered how many agents he must have already met while doing his research. I counted at least a dozen names on the list in his notebook. I have never been one to consider us to be glorified "order takers" in the real estate business, although those people certainly exist. As agents, I think it's incredibly important to add value to the transaction, through our knowledge, perspective, and skills.

So, don't be shy with potential clients. Ask for the business! Sometimes, you might get it.

Consistent Marketing Will Equal Results

Since the onset of my real estate career, I have focused most of my efforts toward online marketing. We launched our first Austin real estate website in 1998, and it has obviously undergone several re-designs since then. Over the past decade or so, I have shifted my efforts more toward social media.

When I am speaking with agents who work for our company, I hear a wide variety of marketing and advertising ideas and questions from them.

One of the most frequent questions that I get when I hear a new idea is, "Do you think it will work?"

My response is almost always the same:

> *In my opinion, pretty much any marketing will work if you are consistent with it.*

I stand behind this statement. The example that I give is standing on a street corner handing out business cards to passing motorists or giving a flyer to everyone who is getting a shopping cart at the grocery store.

Will it get a high return? Probably not.

However, what if you stand on the same corner each day and people begin to think of you as that "out of the box" (or perhaps "fresh out of the asylum") Realtor? I haven't ever tried this personally, but I can virtually guarantee that some sales would eventually come from this technique.

Why is this? Because at any given time, if you take a random sample of 100 people on the street, a handful of them are considering buying or selling real estate.

If your marketing is consistent, you will manage to reach a certain percentage of qualified potential clients with your message each time. If you give up too soon, you won't be able to see the results.

My advice is to stick with your marketing idea, no matter how far off the beaten path it may seem at first.

There was a guy I used to work with who consistently marketed to an area near our office that wasn't interesting to me at all. Over time, this guy became the expert for that pocket of town, and he's done extremely well. I certainly don't resent his success for this, because he was consistent.

How Much Should You Focus Your Marketing?

Some real estate coaches recommend trying to tightly focus your marketing, or to find a niche where you can thrive. I can't promise that I will supply the right answer for you on this, but I can give you some thoughts that may help you decide how to proceed.

You could consider becoming a neighborhood "specialist," mailing information to your immediate area (or any number of specific neighborhoods, for that matter).

As I mentioned earlier, your sphere of influence is comprised of the people who know, like, trust, and remember you. Here are some excellent niches for you to consider:

- Friends from church
- People you meet through a common interest or hobby that you share
- A group of people you know who share the same profession as each other (teachers, lawyers, doctors, etc.)

> **Note:** If you do decide to present yourself publicly as a neighborhood specialist, take it seriously and make sure you know enough to use this title. I'm not saying that you need exhaustive knowledge about every sale, but at least know something about the local schools, where the grocery stores are, and get a few sales under your belt there first. If real estate is a second career or if you're working part-time, you may want to keep your marketing close to home. If you're in a big city, you will want to branch out and cover a larger market area in the meantime, to start getting income while you work on your reputation in your target area.

I once saw an agent using a "SUBDIVISION SPECIALIST" rider sign on her first sale. The home was badly overpriced, and I couldn't even let my buyers purchase that one in good conscience.

When we first bought the domain name for our website in 1998, no one understood what we would even do with it. I am not making this up. Times have changed, and now most buyers start their search for a new home (and most other things) online. This can enable you to work a broad area if you choose this, but sites like Nextdoor can also help you to get your name out there in your neighborhood and in other nearby areas.

If you want to go with geographic marketing, you can also consider starting a Facebook group for the area. If you do this, you need to be prepared to monitor the group and participate there, so don't spread yourself too thin trying to market to too many areas at once in this manner.

If you do consistently market to one area, you should be able reap reliable results over time, but this is a long-term plan, so don't expect fast results. You will probably get some opportunities early, but it takes time to establish and prove yourself and get a good reputation as the default agent for a neighborhood.

Networking—How to Be the Most Popular Person in the Room

When we first started in real estate, we used to spend vast amounts of money on print advertising. It felt like we tried everything: Newspapers, local magazines, national magazines, flyers, mailouts, and more. I felt like much of what we did in that initial year or two provided a quick education on which marketing truly works, and which methods to avoid.

If you want the most "bang for your buck," face-to-face networking is the most effective single strategy you can implement. The good news is that it doesn't have to cost you a cent.

One small step you can take is to actually show up when you're invited to a party, gathering, or just to hang out with friends. When you take the opportunity to discuss your business in an organic way during these gatherings, that alone should bring you several transactions over time.

Here is the best part: When you are in real estate, people *already* want to talk about your business!

If you are a real estate agent or broker, I promise you that most people are interested in how the market is doing in your area. In fact, I've noticed that it often reminds me of the old "E.F. Hutton" commercials from the early 80's (yes, this dates me, but I was a kid back then):

Typically, the scene would start in a crowded restaurant or sporting event. One guy would say to the other, "Well, my broker is E.F. Hutton, and E.F. Hutton says," at which point everyone in the room stops talking to hear what is going to be said. The tagline/motto for the ads was, "When E.F. Hutton talks, people listen."

> ***You can be listened to like E.F. Hutton at any get-together just by virtue of being a real estate professional.***

I think any discussion can be moved into your area of expertise within a few seconds if you are paying attention. However, try to understand that this doesn't give you license to force things. If someone mentions their dead relative, don't say, "Sorry to hear about your dead step-cousin. On another note, the real estate market in Austin is alive and well!"

When I am around friends of friends, or people I barely know, or complete strangers, I sometimes challenge myself to bring real estate into the conversation. Believe me, it's not that hard. If you were an engineer or an accountant, I can assure you that most people wouldn't be that fascinated with your work stories. However, if you're a Realtor, everyone wants to get into your head. They may already own a home, or they may be renting and thinking of buying something soon, or they may want to know if the time is right to invest.

Learn how to be the expert for them!

Chapter 3

Working with Buyers

As I made clear in the first chapter, I enjoy working with buyers. I certainly enjoy selling listings as well, but finding the right place for a buyer is a bit like solving a fun puzzle. I like this challenge.

I have compiled a bunch of tips here for you that I wish I had known when I first started.

I will be covering a lot of ground in this chapter, and there's a good level of detail here. You may need to come back to this chapter to refresh your memory when you're about to meet with a buyer for the first time. I've found that training is usually the most helpful when you're about to use the techniques in real life.

In other words, it's good to read and try to understand this stuff now, but it will be much easier to remember when you know you'll be using it soon. I remember that my first broker taught me all the details about how to write a contract on the day before I met with my first buyer clients.

Getting a buyer to meet with you to look at property is sometimes a big hurdle by itself, so you will want to ensure that your time with your client is as productive as possible. I've met with over 500 buyers in my career, so this is easy for me, but I've also had some hard lessons along the way. I hope you can learn from my experiences.

The very first step when you're working with a new client is to figure out whether they can afford to buy a home in the range you're discussing.

If the buyers are planning to pay cash, you need to get a verification of funds before you spend time showing homes. This is usually given in the form of a printed or electronic bank statement with all their sensitive personal information hidden. On occasion, I have allowed a letter from an attorney or a CPA to serve as proof of funds available. I heavily recommend vetting this as much as you can, mainly because I have personally been burned by fraudulent buyers more than once, resulting in months of wasted effort.

> **Jason's rule of thumb: If they refuse to provide a verification of funds, showing homes to them is a waste of your time and effort.**

Let me expand on that for a second: Imagine that you are looking to buy a home and you have ample cash available to do so. Would you ever be offended if someone asked for proof? I hope not. If you ask for this, and your "client" acts like this is an inconvenience or if they act offended, they probably don't have the money, or at least not yet. I saw this happen a few times early in my career. Please learn from my mistakes. Get something in writing, then verify it to the best of your ability. This is time well spent, I assure you.

If they are planning to finance the home, get them in touch with your preferred lender if possible. You will need a trusted source for mortgage financing, and it's great if you can get buyers to speak with someone you know and like already. If buyers come to you having already chosen a mortgage professional to work with, that's okay. You can still offer to let them speak with your loan officer as well, even if only to compare rates and fees. If they're set on using a specific person that you don't yet know, it's best to take a few minutes to call and speak with him/her to make sure the loan looks solid.

> **TIP: For any first-time buyers (and sometimes for more experienced buyers, too), you may have to push a little harder to get them to go through the qualification process, because they may be anxious to get started looking at homes. If this is the case, I usually explain to them that we want to make sure the numbers make sense, so that *they* don't waste**

> time looking at places outside of their price range. Make it about them, not you. While it's true that it would be a waste of your time as well, you want to put it in terms that they will better accept. As a rule, most people are more protective of their own time than they are of yours.

If they are referred to you through a trusted past client or friend, you can use your judgment about whether you feel comfortable starting the showing process without a loan letter or at least a conversation with their lender, but you normally want to err on the side of caution with this.

> **Exception:** If you know that it's going to be a while before they buy, perhaps because they have a home to sell, or a relocation coming in a few months, or they're cleaning up a couple of credit issues, you could certainly spend some time in person to develop rapport with your newfound potential clients. This will help them to feel more loyal towards you and they'll be more likely to work with you when they eventually buy a home. In these cases, I try to position myself as a resource for any questions they may have, and I tell them I'll be ready to help when the time comes.

When I am trying to help a new buyer, I always start with a few basic questions:

- What price range are you looking at?
- What size home are you hoping to find?
- How many bedrooms/bathrooms?
- Is there an area of town you would prefer? Any commute?
- Is the age of the home important?
- What about schools? Some buyers want "good" schools, which is a little subjective sometimes. Do your best to understand what they want on this; it's going to be specific to the age of their kids. If all the kids are little, elementary school may be the primary concern. If the kids are older, elementary school may

not matter at all.

As you chat with them, you'll start to get a sense of what they're looking for, and any other specific requirements they might have (pool, no pool, no carpet, large lot for kids and space, etc.)

Next, it's time to log in to your local MLS (Multiple Listing Service) and see what you find. Send your clients listings via email that you feel are good matches. You'll find that most buyers these days already have a fairly good sense of what's out there from sites like Realtor.com and Zillow, but sending the listings is a good general practice to demonstrate that you're listening to their needs.

While you are searching, if it becomes obvious that you can't find anything that will meet their needs, you can try adjusting the area or bumping the price up to see what you find. You can then either let them know what you found and see if they're interested in the modified results, or just send them what you found and explain it via email. I always try to honor the criteria they give me, unless it's obvious that they're off track, then I give guidance as needed.

> **Tip: This can help to distinguish you from an average agent. Good agents know how to search correctly to maximize their chances of finding the right property. Average agents will just plug in the price that their client tells them to find. Good agents know that they may need to alter this a little. If it's a buyers' market (lots of homes to choose from, homes sitting on the market longer), don't be afraid to bump the price up a little, because you might have a good shot at negotiating it down to suit your buyer's needs. Conversely, if it's a strong seller's market (little inventory, homes selling virtually overnight), you might want to cap the price a little lower, to give your buyers an opportunity to offer something above the listing price.**

When you do get a chance to meet face-to-face, this is when you will want to present any necessary paperwork.

How to Present and Use Buyer Representation Agreements

I have a method for presenting a buyer's rep agreement (and any other required paperwork) that *works* well for me, and I hope this will work for you, too.

In Texas, we must have any potential buyers sign an "Information about Brokerage Services" form whenever we have any substantive discussions about real estate. This lays out the basics about how various agency relationships work. This may also be the case where you work, or perhaps there is another form that you must use early in the process, either from a state requirement or from your brokerage.

In a nutshell, I suggest presenting all necessary forms upon meeting the client, but don't make them sign the buyer's representation agreement until you have put in a little time and work on their behalf.

Here's the basic script (although it is free-form and you should put it into your own words to make it more effective):

> YOU: I have a couple of forms that I need to show you. One of them is required by the Real Estate Commission, and the other one is for our office files, required by our broker (I let our agents put the blame for this annoying paperwork on me if they want to).

At this point, you can go ahead and briefly explain each document, have them sign the basic information form, then:

> YOU (again): So, since I don't want to assume anything just yet, I won't require you to sign the agreement until we're ready to wrap things up today. That way you'll get a chance to preview the way I work and we can get to know each other, with no obligation on your part. I'll let you keep it to look over as we're driving around.

Before you part ways with the buyers for the day, you can ask if they feel comfortable having you represent them. If you've been out for hours helping, hopefully they will be happy to sign. This method has always worked for me. If someone is unwilling to sign under those terms, you shouldn't waste another second of your time with them. They are simply not worth the effort, and you're just spinning your wheels if you continue.

Showing Properties to the Client

Once you have handled the paperwork, it's time to start looking at homes.

Hopefully, you'll be able to learn a lot about their preferences once you get a chance to view some homes in person together. Often, you will find that what they told you doesn't match up with how they react in person. Maybe they genuinely don't like older homes, though they seemed open to this idea, or they will fall in love with a house that is smaller than they told you they wanted. Go with the flow and help them accordingly.

Here are some tips to keep in mind during your day showing properties.

Set the tone at the outset

I usually say something along these lines, if we have a full day ahead: "We have a sizable number of places to see today. If we pull up to one of them, and you don't like it, just tell me and we'll go to the next place. I want to make the best use of your time. I didn't build these homes, and I don't live in them, so you won't be offending me."

Spend time preparing

Unless there are logistical issues, I try to plan the order of showings geographically.

Part of preparing properly (at least for me) is estimating how long we will spend at each home looking, then calculating drive time, sometimes with traffic thrown in. Here's how I recommend doing that:

1. Once you have a list of homes to show based on your client's needs/wants, pull up all the addresses using your MLS map

feature or Google Maps.

2. If you're picking up your clients at a hotel or at another place where they'll be staying, that's your starting point. Otherwise, choose a home from the list as your starting point. I prefer to use a vacant home for this, just in case one of you is running late. Alternatively, you should choose to prioritize any homes that require firm appointments.

3. Allow a specific amount of time to show each home. If the homes are small, I would allow 10-15 minutes. If they're large, 20-30 minutes each. This is not as easy to predict if it's the first time you're showing this particular client. Side note: If it's a second or third showing and they're considering making an offer, allow a lot more time, but you also may only be looking at one or two places so they can make a final decision.

4. Calculate the estimated travel time between properties, and make sure to consider the time of day just in case you encounter rush hour traffic. Google Maps has a feature that allows you to estimate the travel time based on the specific time of day.

5. Go through your complete list and set up the times accordingly. I try to give a reasonably close estimate on the times, rather than "we're coming this afternoon." I do tell the owner (or agent, or whomever I need to speak with) that we may be a little earlier or later than the window I give initially. Sometimes, you will find out that the seller will be at work or out of town that day, which gives more flexibility.

6. If you're going to be looking all day, always make sure to schedule enough time for lunch. This is "down time," and it gives you and your clients some time to rest and to build more rapport with each other. I try to give some thought to where we can eat lunch in a reasonable amount of time based on where we will be whenever lunchtime hits. The extra thought you put into this will make you look like a true professional.

I prefer to be as prepared as I can when I meet with my clients, because no matter how shiny your shoes are or how nice your car is, your clients will not be impressed if you come across to them as disorganized or ill-prepared.

Often, while I am engaged in the showing process, I hear something along these lines from my clients: "Jason, I'm impressed. You are detailed and organized. Thanks for preparing so thoroughly for our day together. It made things smooth for us."

Even though I have heard this type of thing many times, it still surprises me. I don't consider myself to be overly organized generally — I've just always figured that planning was part of my job as an agent.

Buyers say this more often when they have already met with another agent in the past and become disenchanted with them before we ended up working together: "Wow, the guy we used to buy our last house always seemed like he was sort of winging it. Sometimes, he would just show up at the houses and ask if we could look at them right then."

This strikes me as amazingly disrespectful. The only professional approach is to set up the showings ahead of time, and to give each homeowner a fairly good idea of when we will show up. Certainly, there are extenuating circumstances sometimes, but I usually have a list of properties and I can estimate with some level of certainty what time we will see each one of them. The primary exception occurs when I have a buyer that takes an inordinate amount of time to see each place. I once had a buyer whose dad tagged along, and he insisted on seeing everything (even the attic), even when they were clearly not going to buy that home. I had to gently nip that in the bud.

Spend some time preparing. You will thank yourself.

Be honest

Simply put, not every home is worth considering. If it's sitting next to a wastewater treatment plant with railroad tracks behind it, don't be afraid to point out shortcomings. It's the right thing to do, and you will earn points with your clients for showing integrity.

If you don't know the answer to a question, "I don't know" is a fine response, followed by "I bet we can find out, though."

Note taking

I normally encourage my buyers to take notes if we are looking at more than a handful of properties. Otherwise, you might all forget some minor detail, such as the location of the master bedroom, and have to make another trip. I encourage them to take photos or videos if they seem especially interested, or in order to help remember something specific. Sometimes, when there is enough inventory, I may show properties for two or three straight days (all day) to the same clients, because they are under a time crunch to make a quick decision. People will appreciate and remember the effort!

Know your goal when you start the day

I am willing to spend way more time with buyers if I know that they need to buy something soon and they are prepared to make an offer. If they just want to get a feel for the area, I try to spend less time with them overall, but I'll still be willing to show 3–5 homes to give them an idea of what they can expect for their desired budget, and to develop a loyal client for the future.

I always try to honor my clients' desired price range unless it becomes obvious that they need to increase the budget or expand the area for the search. This is sometimes a learning process for buyers as they realize things simply cost more than they hoped.

Chatting all day

When spending the entire day with buyers, you must learn to be a master of small talk. I can usually keep the conversation flowing for hours just by asking questions and listening, then sharing some stories of my own. I try to find some common ground with them quickly.

I sometimes like to challenge myself by imagining that I am a talk-show host trying to gather as much pertinent information as possible in a short amount of time. Many times, the stories you hear will come in handy during negotiations or in helping to get them to pursue a specific property (e.g. "I remember that you said your grandchildren will be visiting a lot. This would be a great yard/playroom for them.") Think of yourself as Jimmy Fallon (or if you're older, Johnny Carson). Get them talking.

Quick story: I did have one truly awkward outing years ago. The buyer didn't say much all day, and I honestly assumed that he wasn't enjoying himself or that he just didn't like me. Later, he ended up buying two properties from me, totaling over $1.8 million. He just wasn't that talkative initially. After that first day, he was much more open when I saw him, but I honestly thought I had struck out on that first day. It turns out he was simply an introvert. When someone is quiet, it doesn't necessarily mean you have failed.

Another time, I had a high-end client who liked to try to finish my sentences for me. I figured I could put up with almost anything under the circumstances. I got the sale by being patient and, frankly, by talking a bit slower.

> **Important bonus tip: I learned a while back not to speak negatively about a property unless something is genuinely important, like if you notice a family cemetery in the backyard, or if one of the bedrooms is halfway into a sinkhole. I don't mean that I try to hide anything from the buyer at all, but I also don't harp on the negative unless I have a good reason (such as safety, noise, or other things which might affect the value).**

If you are helping them to decide between two properties, and you will be writing an offer on one of them, it is always best to leave the other property as a possibility just in case. *In other words, don't go out of your way to fully eliminate the alternate property just to rush them to make an offer,* or you may find yourself in a quandary later because you just talked them out of the only alternate house.

I usually say something like, "In my opinion, you truly can't make a bad decision between these two places. Either one would be great for you." That way, if the first one doesn't work out, you aren't forced to start over. *Obviously, this method only works if it is the truth,* so keep that in mind as well.

Help them to assess the homes without pushing your opinions too hard on them. If there is nothing glaringly wrong with the house, allow them to like it. I would never advocate for minimizing a real problem, but keep your comments pertinent rather than mentioning more subjective stuff. You won't personally like every single home you sell.

Overall, my advice is to take your cues from the client and not talk too much. I have seen agents talk themselves out of a home sale by not being quiet at the right time. You should allow your clients time and space to think. If they seem actively interested in the property (particularly if it's a couple, or multiple buyers), let them talk to each other without hovering.

It's fine to point out additional good features when there is obvious interest. If they're utterly disinterested, it's best to move on to the next place and save everyone's time. Don't push to see a home in its entirety if it obviously won't work for them. This can make your day more productive, and it may help your buyers to refine their decision more quickly.

Once they have chosen a home to pursue, write it up and work on getting the deal in place.

After you have an actual contract, you'll need to get checks for the earnest money and the option fee (again, I am covering Texas-specific rules here). You will coordinate with the chosen title company to get them the earnest money (normally around 1% of the sales price) so that they can "receipt" the contract and send out copies to all pertinent parties, and you need to get the option fee to the seller or the listing agent within three days. If you don't, per the contract, your option period is not actionable, so this is important.

After you've got an actual executed contract, either you or the buyer will need to schedule the inspection. Normally, you will want to get this done as soon as you can, to allow enough time to get the report back and evaluate and negotiate repairs as needed. I don't recommend ever accepting an option period of less than 7 days when I represent buyers, and 10 days is preferred. For more information on this, you can check out the section "Recommending Inspectors" on page 108.

The Inspection

If you are working with an inspector on a regular basis, you will have a sense of how long it will take him (or her) to complete the actual inspection process. I normally recommend telling the buyers to arrive about 30 minutes from the estimated end of the inspection, so they can hear about any important items that were found. You'll have to arrange this with the inspector, because they don't all work in the same way.

After the Inspection: Negotiating Repairs

Frankly, negotiating repairs is one of my least favorite parts of this business. Sometimes this is easy and painless, but on occasion things go awry and people choose to dig their heels in and fight. When emotion enters the negotiating process, things often go downhill after that, so you need to remain calm and help your clients to do the same.

First, there are a few "big ticket" items, as my inspector calls them:

- Foundation
- Roof
- A/C system and furnace
- Water heater
- Active termites
- Mold

If you're dealing with problems in any of these areas, it's reasonable to expect the seller to fix them or to provide adequate funds to do so.

Beyond that, there are safety issues which could arise. It's reasonable to have these items addressed. After that, you will probably have a series of smaller things that are easier to repair.

Explain to your clients that you and they will review the inspection report once you have it in hand, and then you can develop a list together for the items which are critical enough to get the seller to fix them.

If you have a solid inspector, you may have an awfully long list of small items. Try to counsel buyers not to ask for everything on this list, because you're more likely to get pushback, or even an unpleasant response from the listing agent. Try to consider which items would concern you the most if it were your own purchase, and feel free to express this opinion during your discussion with the buyers.

As I alluded to above, if your clients are getting a good price on the house, remind them of this during the repair negotiations, to keep the proper perspective. Keep the big picture in mind. Do not allow pettiness from either principal party to blow your sale. If you must, as a last resort, you could consider chipping in a small amount of money from your commission to assist with the repairs to make everyone happy. Please read that again. Note that I said this is a last resort, but it is occasionally necessary to keep things on track.

Assuming you get past this point, and beyond your option period, your main goal is to keep your buyers calm and happy and keep them moving forward on financing, if they're getting a loan. Other than that, you should be in touch with the listing agent to collect any necessary repair invoices. You will also coordinate with them to do a final walkthrough just before the closing.

Closing Day

I recommend helping to schedule the closing and facilitating between your clients and the title company. I also recommend attending the closing, where your main job is to provide moral support while the buyers sign a bunch of documents. If you have a closing gift for them, this would be the time to present it, unless you want to visit them afterwards to do so.

For most buyers, I estimate at least an hour for the closing. Assuming you start on time, it won't take much longer than that. If it's faster, which does happen, it's a pleasant surprise.

Consider taking a photo with your clients after they sign, which you can use for marketing purposes. You can share the picture on your social media platform(s) of choice. I normally do, unless it's obvious that my client doesn't want me to, in which case I might post a "BOUGHT" picture of the house instead. You can also send the photo to your clients as a reminder of your happy day together.

After closing, usually within a couple of hours, the transaction will fund (lender's money will come—buyer's money should already be there) and you will get paid.

Congratulations!

Working with a New Home Buyer

I would like to address some terminology and techniques that are specific to representing a buyer on the purchase of a brand-new home. A lot of the stuff I covered above will still apply, but new homes are different enough that I wanted to cover the basics to help you get up and running more quickly.

In our local market, I can represent a buyer client on the purchase of a brand-new home, and my commission will be always be paid by the builder. This is probably true in your market as well, but my comments here are specific to the central Texas area in that regard.

First, I recommend making sure that you promote the fact that you sell brand-new homes as well as resale/existing homes. Educate your friends and acquaintances about this whenever possible and make it part of your initial spiel when you're speaking with potential clients, no matter what they're searching for initially. I say something along these lines:

"Just to be sure you know, I also sell brand-new homes, if you're interested in pursuing that option. It's a big part of our business each year."

I have lost many potential sales over the years because my friends and some clients didn't realize I could help with this, or even that it would be helpful to have an agent.

Tell them these truths: the builder pays your commission, and if they buy with no representation, they will have no one truly on their "side," and the builder will just make a little more money. Sales reps in model homes do not represent the buyer. They are employees of the builder. In this area, our commission is included in the home price, and reputable builders will not give a discount if a buyer shows up with no agent, because they understand that agents bring much of their business and know that good agents make the process smoother. The exception to this rule would be for a fully custom home builder, who will normally just add your commission to the price of the home.

You will need to educate yourself about which builders are the best, and which ones offer a lower quality product. When you're getting started, you can get some of this from your broker or another mentor, or from listening to other agents in your office during meetings. You can also join local agent Facebook groups if you're in a big enough market for this. There is often some valuable information about builders in those groups. I also recommend spending some time visiting model homes and communities and learning more about what they have to offer.

I won't pretend to provide an exhaustive list of what to do when you are representing a new home buyer, but I will cover some of the more important points here.

First, a few important terms to know:

- **"To be built"** — Seems obvious, I hope. This is a home that will be built from the ground up. Your client will have an opportunity to choose a specific lot and floorplan as well as the interior décor.

- **"Spec home"** — This is a home that is either complete or at least underway from a builder. If it is almost finished or truly finished, your client may have an opportunity to negotiate on the price, because builders are usually motivated to sell spec homes to free up the money and get it off their books.

- **"Elevation"** — In building terms, this is how the home looks on the outside in the front. Often, builders will have 3–5 different elevations for the same floorplan. Maybe one has a front porch and one does not, or one has brick while another has stone and stucco.

- **"Base price"** — This is the starting price of a home, with no upgrades included. Sometimes builders use the base price of their least expensive model to advertise a community, such as "homes starting from the $300s," when they have one small home priced at $399,000 with no upgrades. Either way, it's important to note that the base price is helpful, but it's not necessarily an indication of where the price will end up.

- **"Lot premium"** — This is the buyers' cost for the lot, which is added to the base price and upgrades to determine the final sales price. If a lot backs to a greenbelt, or if it's larger or on a corner, there is often a larger premium attached. Not all lots have premiums, but some builders charge premiums for every lot.

- **"Setback"** — This is how far the home must be built away from the front property line. 25 feet is common here for most "normal" neighborhoods. There is commonly a building line which cannot be crossed in the back and on the sides as well.

- **"Design center"** or **"design studio"** — These are common terms that builders use for where buyers will go (and maybe you will join them) to select upgrades and décor items for their home, including flooring, counters, backsplash, light and sink fixtures, etc.

- **"Master-planned community"** — I found this definition on Bankrate.com, and it covers the bases: A master-planned community is a large-scale residential neighborhood with a large number of recreational and commercial amenities, such as golf courses, tennis courts, lakes, parks, playgrounds, swimming pools, and even stores and restaurants. Some master-planned communities may have schools, office parks, large shopping centers and other businesses.

Some builders will put their spec homes in the MLS, and some won't. If your buyers are interested in buying a brand-new home, you will have to do some research outside of the MLS. Locally, we have a couple of good websites for this, and a magazine that is distributed to all Austin-area agents with ads from builders. Even though you will find some information using sources like this, you should call ahead to each builder you plan to visit to make sure the information is correct, especially for spec homes.

If your clients want a to-be-built home, it's important to make sure that they understand the timeline for this. If they want to be in a new house in three months, that is not feasible unless the home is already underway. I have seen homes take 12 months or more. A typical timeline to build is 5–10 months, based on my experience.

Part of your job as the buyer's agent is to help them select a home that makes sense for their family and their needs. This will include both the floorplan and the lot. I try not to sell homes that back up to busy roads or commercial properties, as one example. Most buyers here will end up adding 10–15% to the price in upgrades, so bear in mind that a home which is $400k on a price list might end up at $450–475k after lot premium and upgrades are added. So, if their "all in" budget is $500,000, you should cap your search around $425–450k for the base price.

Once they have selected a builder and the right home and lot, the contract is always done by the builder's salesperson. It's good to know this in advance, since it's different from selling a resale home in that regard. I promise that the contract will be steeped in legalese. It may be a good idea to review this paperwork with your broker if you find any concerns, or just in general, especially when you're starting out.

Some common elements: they are always weighted in favor of the builder, and there is no written promise to complete the home on a specific date. The builder rep will give you an estimated timeline for the construction, but the paperwork will not commit the builder to this timeline. If your buyers balk at this, tell them that it's always in the builder's best interests to move things along promptly.

The full contract takes some time, often hours. Most builders I work with want to get all the structural options figured out before the contract is signed. This will include the elevation, the orientation of the house (garage on the right or left), and other optional items which will become part of the final house plans.

Some thoughts on new home financing: Builders around here usually offer incentives to use their preferred mortgage lender, and they normally do so by offering to cover the title policy and other closing costs. Sometimes, the incentives are huge. For larger homes, if the incentives are smaller, the

buyers may be better served by shopping around or sticking with the lender who got them pre-qualified. Builders' "preferred lenders" often do not offer the absolute best rate, so that they can absorb some of the incentive, and the service is sometimes sub-par, because they are handed so much business that they're not working as hard to get borrowers. However, I have been pleasantly surprised plenty of times by builder lenders who were excellent.

The bottom line for buyers: it may be worth putting up with sub-par service if there's a significant financial incentive to do so. They may need your help to keep this in perspective and act accordingly. I once had a sale that involved $20,000+ given to my buyer clients, but it was contingent on using the builder's lender. That is not a difficult decision to make, clearly.

Once the contract is done, you may have a waiting game for a to-be-built home, while the builder obtains permits. This is normally when the builder will want your client to visit their design studio to make all their décor selections.

It will be a few weeks before anything happens on the lot, then you will see "forms" appear. These are put in place to hold the concrete foundation, which will come after the ground-floor plumbing is put in place.

Your primary jobs throughout the building process are to answer questions and to facilitate communication. You may also be called upon to resolve any disagreements between the buyer and builder should they arise, though these are rare in my experience.

I normally recommend getting an inspection near the end of the process, and you may also wish to suggest a pre-pour foundation inspection and a pre-sheetrock/frame inspection. All of these are third-party independent services, and your buyers would cover the cost.

There will be several walkthrough meetings during the construction process, and one final walkthrough about a week before you close. This last one is done so that the buyers (and you) can look for cosmetic issues or other problems that haven't yet been resolved. I did a final walkthrough once for a gorgeous luxury home where there were 21 outstanding items, so don't be surprised if there are still defects and cosmetic issues that are not resolved, even days before the closing. Good builders will be anxious to get everything done on time.

Just be supportive and available, as always, and offer to follow up as needed. If your clients are out of town, you may need to serve as their "eyes and ears" to finalize things on the day before they close. This is part of providing memorably good service.

Helping Choosy Buyers "Pull the Trigger" with a Contract

Sometimes, you will feel stuck and helpless with clients who struggle to decide about which home to buy, even when they are motivated. Your patience may run low with them, and you'll find yourself wondering if it's even worth continuing. If you're like me, you may get stubborn, and tell yourself, "Well, I've come this far, I might as well see this thing through to the end. I don't want to waste all these hours I've already spent with them." It's best to remain calm and patient.

Once, I was working with an older couple for several weeks as we prepared their home for sale and simultaneously looked for a new place for them. They wanted to leave their neighborhood of 30+ years and move out of the city. They reported feeling a little unsafe in their current home, so the decision to move was not a difficult one. As with many older neighborhoods, theirs was one that had gone downhill, and they wanted to leave.

At any rate, as I was working with them and we were evaluating possible places to move, the wife produced a virtual avalanche of questions, presumably from her fear of selling after living in one place so long. As I patiently answered every question, I thought, "Will they ever commit to a home?" It seemed unlikely for a while, because their needs/wants seemed to be difficult to find for their desired price range. Then one day while we were looking at homes in Georgetown, we struck gold.

Even though we found the perfect property, they needed to see it again. Then they needed to see it once again with their kids and grandkids. Then they needed to think about it for several more days.

Obviously, I was incredibly pleased when I finally got a call from the husband asking me to come over that evening and prepare an offer. I happily obliged, arriving at the appointed time. His wife was just getting home when I showed up, and she greeted me, and we began to chat a little bit. She suddenly asked me, "So, what are we doing tonight?"

Unfortunately, he had not bothered to tell her that I was there to write an offer on the house they wanted.

Needless to say, this was an awkward way to start the offer process.

They talked about it at length in front of me, and then she began again with her typical litany of questions:

1. What happens if we don't sell our current home?
2. What do you think they will accept as a sales price?
3. What happens during the inspection if they find something wrong?
4. Why is the HOA fee so high?
5. How tall are you?
6. What is your blood type?
7. Where did you go to school?
8. What is your favorite color?

Okay, I was kidding. Two of those questions didn't come up during our time together.

As I was sitting there, absorbing her questions and explaining the process in great detail, I remembered an old sales script I had seen somewhere years ago, called the "Important Decision" close.

I said simply, "I know that this is a major decision for you. Is there anything else that you need from me before we get started?"

As you may already know, part of any good closing question is silence. In other words, it is best to keep your mouth closed and simply wait for a response. If you start speaking too quickly, it can defuse the power of the moment.

She sat thinking for what seemed like a minute or more (which is a long time to sit quietly), then she simply said, "I guess not. Let's write it up."

Wow!

This was a huge turning point, but I had to shut my mouth to make it happen.

My client was relieved and so was I, frankly. Keep this one in mind if you ever have an indecisive client. Having a client paralyzed by inertia is not fun for anyone.

MAKING THINGS RIGHT

When things go awry, it's critical to make them right to the best of your ability. You can't control everything in a transaction, but you can control how you react.

About eight or nine years ago, I sold a home in Leander before it went on the open market. It was a rare case when I was representing both the buyer and the seller. Both had been referred to me through different loan officers in Houston, which was also unusual.

I met with the seller and gave her a realistic price for her home, and she planned to list it with me. Before we listed it on the MLS, the buyers wanted to meet and look at homes in that area. I asked the seller if I could show the home, and she agreed. Surprisingly, that was the buyers' favorite from the 4-6 places I showed, so we wrote a contract.

Things proceeded relatively smoothly until the closing day, when I was scheduled to meet with each party separately for their respective closing appointments at the title company. I had offered to do a final walkthrough on the house with the buyers before any of this occurred, and they didn't seem interested. However, they did go to the house to park one vehicle there before the closing.

As the seller was finishing, I looked through the glass door into the lobby and saw that the buyers were there waiting. I decided to go greet them, and I made the mistake of asking the seller if she wanted to meet them. She came with me.

You will soon understand why this became incredibly awkward.

As I went into the lobby, I saw the buyer sitting with his arms crossed, scowling at the floor. This is not the body language you want to see from someone who is about to finalize his home purchase. His wife was beside him, looking distressed, but kind. Let's call them John and Ellen.

I greeted him by name and asked how he was doing (though it was not hard to decipher that he was unhappy).

JOHN: "Not good. Not good at all. I went by the house, and there was a lot of trash at the curb, and there's still a wreath on the door. I don't think she cleaned her stuff out."

ME: "Well, the trash is not unusual during a move-out. I think she has cleared it out." (turning to the seller, standing next to me) "You got it cleaned up and got your stuff out, right?"

SELLER: "Right. I left a couple of things I thought they could use. I still need to go by and get my cat on my way out of town."

JOHN (to me, not acknowledging the seller directly): "I don't want her in the house."

ME: "Well, technically she still owns the house until the transaction funds, which will happen after you sign."

My statement was the proverbial straw that made it impossible for John to hold it together. I am still amazed at what happened next: He just got up and walked out the door and kept walking.

The seller decided to leave to go get her cat from the house, then she was planning to go immediately out of town to Dallas to her son's house.

I asked John's wife where their car was parked, and she pointed to it, just outside the door. John was not in the car.

ME: "Any idea where he might have gone?"

ELLEN: "No. He was just really mad."

ME: "I guess I should go look for him. Do you think he's mad at me?"

ELLEN: "Well, I don't think he would hit you."

The thought that he would hit me had never even crossed my mind.

I did go look for John. I walked around the building and when I returned, I saw him walking away along the sidewalk about 1/3 of a mile from the office.

I told Ellen, "I will go to the house and check on things and I will call you and let you know how things look, then you can decide about the signing."

She liked this idea, so off I went.

As I was arriving to the neighborhood, I saw the seller leaving in her car, but we didn't talk.

When I got to the house, I discovered that John was right! The trash wasn't a concern, nor was the wreath, but the seller had left a ridiculous amount of stuff in the house. There was a breakfast table and four chairs, a bookcase, a large chair and ottoman in the living room, a large computer desk in the back bedroom, a large tube TV, a hamper, stuff on the back patio, and lots of junk in the garage, some useful, and some not.

She also did not clean the carpets, which she had agreed to do. The house was warm inside and smelled like cat urine.

I called my business partner, Frank Cavitt, who picked up a U-Haul truck and brought it to the house. I also called a local carpet cleaning company, and they were able to send someone out quickly.

I called the title company and spoke to them and to John (who had returned). I told him the truth about the condition of the house, and I told him that I would handle getting everything out and getting the carpet cleaned for them. I told him I would call him when I was finished and he could come see it, then sign the papers.

While we were still unloading the garage, and while the carpet cleaners were still there, John and Ellen showed up.

ME: "Hey John. We're getting all of this junk out. I'm so sorry this happened. As you can see, we got a lot of stuff onto the truck already. When we finish, you can go back and sign."

JOHN: "We already signed everything. When you told me you would handle it, I already knew you would make it right. I trust you."

I was touched by his comments, and by the fact that he had complete faith in me to make this situation right for him. He later wrote an unprompted review online for me, raving about what a great agent I was.

This was one of the most memorable situations when I realized that my firm commitment to run my business with integrity had paid off. Make this a habit, keep your promises, and you will not be sorry.

ACTIVE LISTENING

> **Note: Before you decide to skim this section, which may appear at first glance to only be a story about a local restaurant, please know that it has a valuable real estate message. Listening is a critically important skill.**

I took my family to Red Lobster one Sunday after church. The food there was great, but the service was not perfect. You may have noticed a disturbing trend these days with waiters and waitresses—they often *don't write stuff down*.

Is this supposed to impress me somehow? As if I would say, "Wow, honey, did you notice that the guy didn't write down any of our complicated order? I mean, there are six of us here. If he gets it right, I think we should double his tip."

I normally tip well, because I used to be in restaurant management in the mid-90s, so I know how hard the average waitperson works. However, when my order is messed up, I get more perturbed if they didn't write it down initially. It makes me assume that they weren't paying attention. Of course on that Sunday, the waitstaff ended up looking negligent by forgetting many of our family's special requests.

As I alluded to earlier, listening is a critical sales skill for *any* service provider, and the same goes for us in the real estate and mortgage industries.

In 2003, I got my first sale over the $1 million mark. The buyers were from New York, and they had worked with me several years earlier, then "put things on hold" because they couldn't find what they wanted. They resurfaced in 2002, wanting to know if I was still willing to help. It turned out that they had worked with two other agents for long stretches of time while searching for the perfect place. They told me that they had always found me to be trustworthy, so they returned to let me assist them.

I managed to find the right home on their first visit, and they closed on that home for over $1 million.

What did I do differently?

I wrote down the buyer's list of needs/wants. Believe me, it was a long list. After I had combed through all the listings, it was apparent that there was just one place that I thought would work for them, and it turned out that I was correct. They are still living in that house today.

I have had countless buyers tell me something along these lines during my career: "The last agent we tried to work with didn't pay attention to us. She showed us what she thought we would like, rather than what we actually wanted to see."

Pay attention to your clients! It pays off.

I have mentioned this quote in the past, and I don't know the source, but I have never forgotten it:

> **God gave us two ears and one mouth for a reason.**
> **We should listen twice as much as we speak.**

Don't be the pushy fool who loses an existing client by showing them the wrong homes. Listen to them (and write important stuff down) and reap the benefits.

"Should We State a Deadline to Respond to Our Offer?"

I've received the question above dozens of times from buyer clients I've helped, so I wanted to make sure to cover this topic. Whenever I write up an offer for a home, there are so many questions that come up during the process before we even submit the paperwork to the listing agent. This question typically arises after we've parted ways, and everything is signed.

So, is it a good idea to place a "fuse" on your offer, forcing a quick response?

In my humble opinion, it's rarely necessary to do so, although I can understand arguments in favor of this strategy.

My normal response is this: You certainly can restrict the timing for acceptance by forcing the seller to respond quickly (e.g. "Seller to respond by 5pm Tuesday, January 25th, or this offer is void,") but it comes across as pushy in most cases. A typical seller is sufficiently motivated to respond quickly anyway unless they're traveling or experiencing a crisis of some sort.

Give some thought to the message it sends when you opt to place a deadline on any offer. It might set the wrong tone during negotiations and possibly the entire process, depending on the personality of the seller. It also could come across as a little desperate or weaken the offer and your leverage. Patience is sometimes your friend when it comes to negotiating.

There are only two instances which immediately come to mind under which I would counsel someone to use a deadline approach:

- You're fairly sure that there's another offer (or more than one) on its way the next day, or
- You have a limited amount of time to choose a home, and there's a solid backup house your clients have in mind that you don't want to lose while you wait for a response

Additional Tips for Buyer's Agents

Don't be afraid to write up an offer well below the asking price if it seems halfway reasonable. There are times when it's obviously the wrong move, but you might be surprised by the reaction. Don't be shocked to get a pseudo-offended response, followed by a solid, workable counteroffer. Some listing agents like to act upset on behalf of their clients, then present the offer.

Tell your clients the truth as you see it. If you think a home they want will sell at or above the asking price, tell them so.

As I see it, your job is to help your clients get the home they want/need at the best price possible. You don't have to push and argue and squeeze every dime out of the transaction when negotiating, assuming the property is already a solid purchase/investment.

You won't win any big points with a listing agent by sending over a list of comparable sales or some other justification for your price. Just tell them that this is what your clients were comfortable paying and leave it at that. If you can say it honestly, you have leverage. There's no need to be pushy.

If you must chip in a little bit of your own commission to make the deal work, do it, but *only if you have no choice.* I once gave up $3,000 toward repairs after we hit a stalemate. My eventual commission check on that sale was $84,000. No-brainer, right? Think about your priorities and don't let your pride get in the way.

While I don't think being overly prideful is the way to build your business, you can gently remind your clients of the work you have done for them (e.g. "I think this was a productive day of showings." or "I'm happy to see that my technique/idea worked well, and I'm happy to see the price you got on this place.")

Chapter 4

Working with Sellers

When I first started in this business, I heard the phrase "list to last" so many times in my training that I wondered if I should even try to get buyer clients. This was intended as a motivational training phrase for new agents to demonstrate that to be successful in real estate, it's important to list homes. While there is some measure of truth in this phrase, I've seen many agents who have had long careers working almost exclusively with buyers, especially selling new-construction homes. I recommend working with buyers and sellers both, because it gives you a balanced sense of the market, and because there's no good reason to turn down an opportunity to make money.

I want to give you some basic training here, as well as some more nuanced guidance for when you are a listing agent.

First things first…

QUICK STEPS TO DOING A CMA (COMPARATIVE MARKET ANALYSIS) FOR A HOME

Congratulations! You got a call from someone wanting to sell their home, and you secured the appointment. Before you head over to see the house, you need to spend some time researching the comparable sales ("comps") to have a good sense about the best price for your potential listing.

If the home is in a neighborhood with a good number of recent sales, this is easy to accomplish in your MLS, using the following criteria:

1. Pull up all active and pending listings in the neighborhood, along with the sales for the past 90–120 days. If it's a newer

subdivision, the legal description of the area should be simple to determine. For older areas, you may need to do a map-based search (maybe pulling everything within a half mile of the subject property).

2. "Bracket" the square footage for the house. This is an appraisal term which means you try to use comps that are closest in size to your potential clients' home. As an example, if the house were 2,250 square feet, you should include everything from 2,000–2,500 s.f. or so. Adjust the value for differences in size, but not if the homes are within 100 s.f. This is negligible for this purpose.

3. Try to limit the comps to homes with the same number of stories. This should give you a more accurate sense of the value.

4. Adjust the value for things like extra garages, larger or smaller lots, age, etc. If a home has a substantial improvement (like a pool), I adjust this at around ¼ to ½ the cost of installing one. Currently, I would add at least $25,000–$30,000 if a home has a pool, all other things being equal. If it's a luxury home, this might add $50,000. If you have a third garage bay instead of only two, I would add $10–15k. An extra bedroom is worth a similar amount if you go from 3 to 4, but probably not if you go from 4 to 5. A four-bedroom home is considered large normally, and there's not as much value for extra bedrooms beyond that in my experience.

I take some printed sheets that I can leave with the sellers, and I try to include enough details about the other homes (photos, etc.) that they can see that my suggested price makes sense.

If there are not enough recent sales to choose from in the immediate area, you should expand the search until you have enough. I would recommend first expanding geographically a little. If this gives you some data to work with, move forward. If not, try going back 180 days within the more immediate area and see what the results are.

For more specialized properties (waterfront, ranches, high-end luxury homes), it may be a little trickier to establish a solid value. For a ranch property, expect to use a much wider search area to find something similar.

The more homes you list, the better your ability will be to determine the right price.

As a general rule, keep in mind that there are lots of "breaking points" regarding real estate prices. Here are the current breaking points (my term) as I see them in our local market, just to give you a sense of what I am talking about. These are some good example ranges that typical buyers will consider:

- Up to $250,000
- Up to $300,000
- $250,000–$350,000
- $300,000–$400,000
- $400,000–$500,000
- Up to $600,000
- Up to $750,000
- Up to $800,000
- Up to $900,000
- Up to $1,000,000
- $1–2 million
- $2–4 million
- "The sky's the limit"

That last category may or may not be true, but someone searching for a home above $4 million is typically not overly concerned if it costs a lot more. Those are rare in my local market, but your market may be different.

Regardless, buyers normally have an upper limit in mind when they're searching for a home. Taking the above list into account, it's important to note that if their high number is $500,000, they may not be willing to look at a home priced at $509,000, or they may not find it in the first place because of the search parameters they're using. Strive to have a good understanding of the various breaking points for buyers. You can also look at various online portals to see which price ranges they use.

To clarify further, it's important to note that a person who finds your listing priced at $509,000 may be comparing it to homes that are up to $550,000 or even $600,000, so this may not be favorable to you or your clients. If it is priced at $500,000, your competition may be at $465,000 and yours will shine in comparison.

I cannot overstate the importance of pricing a home correctly.

You're Going to a Listing Appointment? How to Win Almost Every Time

Over the years, I have attended hundreds of listing appointments. These days, it seems like I'm competing less and less often, since the sellers probably found me through a friend of mine or a past client, or perhaps we've worked together before. At any rate, I have a few tips I've developed which may help you during your own appointments.

- **Be Honest** — You will notice this as a theme throughout my book. This is the primary key to success in the listing arena. Sometimes this includes revealing some more painful truths, such as the need for changing décor choices or making necessary repairs. You can also enlist the help of a professional stager on some of these items.

  The hardest part is being direct and upfront about pricing (please see the preceding section), especially when it might mean that they will lose money on their home, or if they have a preconceived notion about how much they will profit. However, it is much easier to have these conversations before the home goes on the market. Otherwise, you may find the house sitting for a long time, then be forced to have a much more difficult discussion about reducing the price or changing something else.

- **Don't Use a Canned Speech** — I have never been one to use PowerPoint slides or force a potential client to endure a long spiel of mine. Do you enjoy hearing a preprepared sales speech when you're buying something? Probably not. Neither will your clients.

- **Set the Tone and Bring Data** — Upon arriving at the home, I usually ask them if I can put my book and folder somewhere while we look around the house. When we sit back down, I tell them that I've brought some information that I plan to leave with them, and some info about comparable sales.

  I also tell them that I don't have a planned presentation (see above), which tends to make them more relaxed. I have a conversational style and I may spend more time than most agents just listening and "interviewing" the sellers in order to understand their goals. This has served me well, and I would encourage you to spend more of your time with sellers listening and developing rapport, and less time talking about yourself (unless they're asking, of course).

- **Be Confident**—If you are confident (or if you aren't), it shows. When I started in real estate, I had no problem listing luxury homes even though I was in my mid-20's. Why? Confidence, even if it might have been misguided. Many times back then, I was just winging it, and they may have realized that, but my willingness to look them in the eye and be direct and forthright even when I didn't have all the answers worked wonders. I haven't ever stopped doing this.

- **Go the Extra Mile**—I can promise you that most other agents will not offer to do this, but I've found that clients respond well when you offer to show them their current competition. Put them in your car and show them the homes that are for sale nearby. Sometimes, that's all it takes to get them to a more realistic place when it comes to pricing and condition. I've often said something like, "We can certainly try your price, but we'll have to wait until (the better priced) home sells before yours will." No one wants to think they will have to wait.

- **Tell Them How It Is**—This may sound like more advice about being honest, and it is, but in a more detailed way. If I know there are three other agents competing for their business, many times I will leave a parting comment such as, "Whatever you do, don't choose an agent based on the listing price they give you. Just because someone says your home is worth more, that doesn't make it correct. The market sets the price, not any individual agent." In a strong seller's market, you can explain that they are likely to get the maximum market value, even if you do underprice it a little bit.

- **Don't Be Afraid to Turn One Down**—Sometimes, taking a listing simply doesn't make sense, either because of the pricing or because you get a bad feeling, or for some other reason. If this is the case, you don't have to be abrupt. I usually say something like, "Because of (reasons), I don't feel like I would be the best agent to market your home." Typically, this is because of the price, but it could be something else altogether.

- **If You Don't Get the Listing, Be a Class Act**—On the occasions when I have lost a listing to someone else, I always react in roughly the same way. I simply say, "I'm sorry to hear that. I hope things work out well with your agent. If not, please keep me in mind." Sometimes, I end up as their listing agent anyway after they become dissatisfied with the agent they chose over me, because I didn't act offended or upset.

I hope you found this list of tips helpful. This is not an exhaustive list, but it should provide a good start.

Using Your Powers of Observation to List More Homes

When I am on a listing appointment with someone I haven't met before, I try to glean as much information as possible about the sellers while they are showing me around the property. This is not to be sneaky; it just helps to find points of commonality.

Here are a few ideas that have worked well for me over the years:

- What types of books are on their bookshelves (assuming they have them)? Maybe they're huge Stephen King fans, or maybe they're do-it-yourself enthusiasts. Maybe all their books are sci-fi novels, or maybe they have 20 Bibles. Whatever the case, you can tell a lot about people by what they choose to read, or at least by what they choose to display.

  I love scanning the bookcases a bit when we're touring the home. Later, when we're discussing the market analysis, I can mention casually that "I noticed you have that book by (author) about (topic)." If I've read it, we have an instant connection. If I haven't, but I'm interested, I'll ask for a brief review from them.

  You could do the same thing with other forms of entertainment, but as we move toward more streaming movies and music, and more books on electronic devices, this is tougher to do than it used to be.

- What's on their fridge? Is it photos of their kids? Photos of them? Menus from favorite restaurants? Vendors they've used in the past? Whatever the case, you can probably learn a little about them and what they value by looking here.

Obviously, I am not advocating that you alter your priorities or your personality to suit the situation like a chameleon, but I think it's fine to notice things you might have in common with them.

- What's on the walls? Often, you will see something that you can latch onto and talk about (interesting artwork, sports memorabilia, their wedding picture, and so on.)
- Pay attention and you will reap the benefits. Maybe you share a love of the same sports team or artist. If you want to score a few extra points, take note of some small repair or cosmetic item in need of work while you are touring the home, then bring it up casually during your discussion with them. This is not meant to put them on the defensive, but to show that you know this business and you understand what it takes to get a house sold.

Don't ever be afraid to be upfront and honest about decluttering or cleaning the home. Top agents all understand this—that's one reason they're top agents!

Consider getting the home professionally staged. If you can find a good stager in your budget, I would highly encourage you to do this. Frankly, it may be less necessary when inventory is tight and buyers are just scrambling to find something, but it's always good to put your best foot forward.

Outside of choosing an agent, remember that the two main factors the seller can control are price and condition. Once you have the home in good showing condition, make sure to price it correctly.

If the home is already in pristine condition, just price it right and work on getting the listing agreement signed!

After the house is ready to be shown to buyers, the first call you should make is to your trusted local real estate photographer—one of the best assets you should have in your arsenal. I've been using the same photographer since 2008, because he's reasonably priced and incredibly talented. I use him for every property I list now, including lease properties. Paying a pro to take pictures is a smallish thing that every agent should do, but many still don't.

You'll need to work with your clients to determine how you will handle scheduling showings with buyers. From my discussions with other agents and brokers around the country, I know that there's a wide variation on this topic: some areas prefer to use a third-party online showing service which helps with scheduling, while other agents prefer that you call them directly so that they can arrange everything. If I have a vacant listing, I just put a lockbox there and allow agents to show it anytime without an appointment. If there is some compelling reason not to do this (such as an alarm or gate code), I have them call or text me for this information.

> **Side Note about Surveys:** When you are on the verge of listing a house, be sure to check with the sellers to see if they have an existing survey in hand. On the off chance that you are not familiar with surveys, they are essentially maps of the property, showing where all the property lines are, and where the house sits (unless it's raw land, of course). The survey will include any pertinent building/setback lines, easements, and all the structures on the property.
>
> If the seller has the survey in hand already, it will save many hundreds of dollars for them later, since most buyers (at least in our market) want the seller to provide this, and escrow companies will need it for the closing. Surveys don't really expire, and I have seen surveys that were 30+ years old used for closings. A survey is typically valid if it's legible, no permanent changes have been made which would affect the survey, and it includes the surveyor's seal. Sometimes, title companies will allow sketches

> for expanded patios or other changes. From my understanding, this is because these companies rarely have claims related to the survey, so they've become much more lenient about this.

With or without the survey, you will now move forward with listing the home in your MLS, based on the timing that you will establish with the sellers. Spend some time to make sure that the listing is thoroughly completed there, because you never know what criteria might bring the right buyer. It could be something that seems unimportant to you, like whether the house has plantation shutters or a double oven.

It's important to note that 78% of homes sell from the MLS listing being found online by the buyer or by the buyer's agent (50% buyer, 28% agent). Around 7% of buyers still come from yard signs, believe it or not. This is based on a 2018 profile of buyers and sellers from the National Association of Realtors.

Keeping this data in mind, you know you have a good chance of capturing the buyer through some combination of the MLS listing and a yard sign. I recognize that this seems rudimentary, and it is.

With that knowledge, your marketing efforts should be focused mostly on setting the price correctly and then presenting the property in the MLS in a manner that will garner the maximum number of showings. If you have the correct price and great photos, you will get showings and you will sell the house. It's that simple. There are lots of other expensive and/or time-consuming things you could do to market the house if you want, but I recommend sticking with these basic techniques.

For luxury listings, or for some unique properties (ranches come to mind), the sellers may want you to get documentation from each buyer to make sure that every person who views the property is qualified. While I am willing to do this in some cases, I do not recommend allowing this for most homes, because it's not common practice, at least in our local market. The exception would be if you are showing the home yourself to an unrepresented buyer. In that case, you don't want to waste their time or your own, so it is perfectly acceptable to pre-screen them, at least with some questions about their financing. Otherwise, trust your colleagues to do this work ahead of time with any buyers they choose to bring.

Assuming things go well, you will find a ready, willing, and able buyer quickly.

If the house is sitting on the market longer than you expected, make sure to get feedback from the agents who have shown the house to see if they can provide any insight to help you and your clients make adjustments as needed. If you're using a lockbox, you can usually get information about who has shown the house by using a website or phone application created for this purpose. Your broker and/or your local board can provide more direction on this process.

Multiple Offers

If you get a flurry of showings and multiple offers, you should set a deadline for "highest and best" (or "best and final") offers from everyone. Bear in mind that even two offers creates a "multiple" offer situation. I am normally upfront about the number of other offers, and this has served my clients well. I also never lie about the presence of other offers. This is bad form and I have seen it backfire on other agents. Don't play games with your client's property like this. Just be upfront and equitable with buyer's agents.

When you do have several offers in hand for your listing, if several them seem similar, your clients will look to you to provide expertise to distinguish between them and determine which one to accept. Make sure to read each one carefully before you present them to the seller.

Here are some of the factors you can use other than price alone to decide which offer makes the most sense for your clients:

- **Type of financing**—Clearly, an all-cash offer with proof of funds is the most desirable method of purchasing for a seller. All other things being equal, you should take this one. If it's not cash, I would normally give more weight and preference to an offer with a large down payment.

- **Closing costs** — I have been the frequent recipient of offers that are full price, only to discover that the buyers are requesting thousands of dollars in closing costs paid by the seller on their behalf. Pay close attention to the entire contract.
- **Who pays what** — For resale homes here in Texas, the seller normally pays the title policy. Sometimes, creative buyer's agents will recommend that their clients accept this expense in order to make their offer more competitive.
- **Warranty** — I have seen this make the difference in a multiple offer situation. One buyer asked the seller to pay for this, and the other did not. These are normally $450–600 or so.
- **Timing for the closing** — If your sellers want to close quickly, an offer that enables them to do this will be more desirable. Conversely, if they have a specific closing date for a new home, they may want a particular closing date for their current home and they may need to lease it back from the buyers after closing. This is often where negotiations can get derailed.
- **Other requests** — If one buyer is not requesting anything special (non-realty items, like the washer and dryer, for example) and another one is, this could be a consideration. Of course, you can also remove this in your counteroffer.

> **Very Important: Do not give counteroffers to multiple buyers, especially in writing. If they all happen to accept your counteroffer, you have just agreed to sell the house to more than one party and created more than one contract, and this creates a big legal problem.**

Contract to Closing Process as a Listing Agent

After you have an executed contract, either you or the buyer's agent will need to send a copy to your preferred title/escrow company. Coordinate for the buyer's agent to get the earnest money to them and ensure that you get the option money delivered to the seller or to you within three days. Once you or they have this in hand, send a signed receipt page to the buyer's agent.

One of the first things you should expect is for the buyer's agent to let you know when the inspection is scheduled. This process will take several hours to complete, even for a smaller home. There is nothing good that will come from the seller being home during this, so make sure to tell your clients that they should be out of the house while the inspector is there. Buyers usually feel uncomfortable if the sellers are there. Sellers also sometimes say things they shouldn't about the condition of the house or make a promise they later decide to rescind. Make them leave the house for a while.

Inspection Repair Request

Try to prepare your clients ahead of time and let them know they may have repairs to do after the inspection is complete. Even the most well-maintained home will probably have something wrong with it.

If you get a list of requested repairs, review it on your own, then review it with your clients. If there is anything on the list that seems really big (roof leak, foundation issue, A/C not working properly, etc.), you may have to coach the sellers that this is something they'll need to deal with no matter who buys the home, so it's probably best to just bite the bullet and do it for the first contract, rather than starting over.

If the items are smaller or less critically important, you may be able to remove some of them from the list or give a credit from the seller toward the buyer's closing costs, rather than fixing everything before closing. This is a lovely and clean solution many times, if the buyers feel that the amount given is fair and adequate to cover everything they need/want.

If the house commanded full price or even more, this would be a good time to remind the sellers of that fact, if they're being stubborn about repairs. If the sellers give a sizable concession on price, I typically mention upfront to the buyer's agent that the sellers will be less likely to negotiate much at all on repairs unless it's something major.

Moving Toward Closing

After you have determined which items the seller will be responsible for repairing, you can relax a little bit, because that was a big hurdle to clear in your transaction. The rest of the time before closing will be spent checking in with the buyer's agent to ensure things are moving smoothly with the loan (if there is one) and making sure the sellers get the agreed-upon repairs completed. You will need to collect invoices from them and share those with the buyer's agent.

Just before closing, the buyer's agent may want to do a walkthrough with the buyers to make sure things look good before they sign the final papers. Coach your clients to have the house clean and ready for this walkthrough.

For the actual closing, you should attend, as this gives you one more opportunity for some "face time" with your clients, and you can also give them a closing gift if you want. Seller closings do not take very long (maybe 15–20 minutes). Normally, the funding will occur within an hour or two of signing, and that's when everything is "official."

As I mentioned earlier for when you attend closings with buyers, you should consider taking a photo with your sellers for marketing purposes.

Smell Your Way to Success

I remember doing a paper in college about the olfactory sense, which is the technical name for our sense of smell. The olfactory sense is the most closely linked to your memory, and it is some 10,000 times stronger than your sense of taste. Additionally, certain scents will produce a highly emotional reaction. You can probably think of at least one perfume or cologne that reminds you of someone in your past.

Why is this important in real estate? Read on.

I have shown several thousand homes to home buyers over the course of my real estate career. Patterns emerge, and trends occur with buyers. When buyers are looking at a good number of homes, I have found it helpful and natural to designate each home with a shorthand of some sort:

- "The house with the skyline view"
- "The one with the tile roof"
- "The place with the incredible landscaping"

Of course, all of these are positive attributes, right? On the flip side of the coin, think about how it would make you feel if your home received one of these descriptions (all of these are real, from buyers I have worked with):

- "The dog pee house"
- "That house with the funky smell"
- "The stinky house"
- "The pungent food aroma house"

It's not as appealing, is it? It probably won't surprise you to learn that the dog pee house didn't make the top three for my buyers.

All homes have some sort of scent/odor, so it's hard to make it completely neutral. Sometimes, the scent is too strong in the other direction (i.e. it smells heavily perfumed, which can be equally distracting). The worst possible combination is when there is a bad smell that is clearly (though not completely) covered with an air freshener:

- "Is that rotten laundry smell with a hint of lavender? Ahhhhh ... nice."
- "WOW! Is that damp mustiness and lemon freshness combined? I like it!"
- "Lovely vanilla dog scent in the bedroom!"

No one says these things. You must eliminate the source, not just spray Febreze and call it a day.

Make sure you tell your clients about this, and if you notice any off-putting odors, try to determine the source and get it corrected.

We tend to get used to the smell of our own home, which is why it is sometimes jarring to sleep in another house when visiting relatives or friends. If you are wondering if your home has a distinct smell, I recommend going outside for a few minutes and then coming back in. The results may surprise you. This method sort of cleanses your nasal palate, so to speak, and you may discover a problem that you didn't realize existed.

When you have a home listed, you want it to have either a clean scent or something that could evoke a positive memory. Real estate trainers the world round recommend a vanilla scent, or that of freshly baked bread. Take it from me: when you are trying to sell a home, smells do matter. You want buyers to focus on the granite counters, or the high-end flooring upgrades, or designer paint colors, not the cat box.

TOP 7 COMMON MISTAKES TO AVOID WHEN LISTING A HOME

Part of our job is to prevent our clients from making costly mistakes. Some common errors result in having a listing on the market too long, or it may keep a home from selling at all. I've taken the time to record some of the most common errors here for your benefit. This section is not intended to include an exhaustive list of important items when selling a home, of course.

Overpricing

You should know this already, and you probably do, but the listing price is incredibly important. One of the best ways to prevent a home from selling quickly, or at all, is to list it too high. I'm sure that you don't enjoy paying too much for things, and neither do potential buyers of your listing.

This is a sensitive issue for many sellers because we tend to identify with our homes. Many people think of their homes as an extension of themselves and their lives. This is partially true, because our homes are the places where some of the most notable events of our lives occur: the baby's first steps, hugs and time with family, cooking and family meals, holidays, etc.

While this attitude is understandable, when it comes time to sell the home, it's necessary to take a different view. A home sale is a legal and a business transaction. Your clients will value their own home highly, and they may even still see it as "basically new." Buyers who are looking for a home in excellent condition in a convenient location at a reasonable price may see things differently.

Keep in mind that market value is determined by what a motivated and qualified buyer is willing to pay for the home, not simply what the sellers feel it should be worth.

Neglecting Necessary Repairs

I have had clients who want to get everything perfect before selling, which is a problem in and of itself because it can cause expensive delays, but more often as agents we see deferred maintenance items on homes that we are looking to list.

"Wait. What the heck is deferred maintenance, Jason?"

This means that sellers are saving money short-term by allowing things to remain broken, but when it's time to sell, it's suddenly time to fix these items. It's best to put yourself in the buyer's shoes for a moment—would you like to buy a home with problems that the seller refused to fix? Perhaps if it was priced well under market, otherwise no.

Another common trait among sellers we have worked with over the years is the idea that you have negotiated a fair price, so the buyer shouldn't ask for any repairs. Again, try to put yourself on the other side of the deal. While there's a chance the buyer is thinking this way, the more likely scenario is that they want the right price and the best possible condition.

Neglecting to Stage the Home

This one is certainly more difficult in some cases than in others. Occasionally, I see homes that are "showing ready," but usually they need some help preparing to show the place to actual potential buyers. First, tell your clients to declutter! They may be able to throw away a lot of things, or they may need to rent a storage unit, or possibly both if the clutter is serious. Regardless, this is more important in a buyer's market. You may wish to hire a professional home stager (highly recommended if you can find a good one). This can often make the difference in getting more showings and more offers.

As a side note, you want to make the home as neutral as possible, to appeal to the broadest possible spectrum of buyers. Home builders have known this "secret" for years, which is why they hire professional decorators to assist with the design and staging details.

Sellers should be prepared to eliminate any odd décor items that might appeal to their unique sense of style but may appear strange to buyers.

Allowing Sellers to Get Hung Up on Small Stuff

I worked on a ranch sale years ago that was a $7.1 million transaction, and it was almost wrecked over the deer feeders, which cost $1,000–2,000 total. The seller made a handshake promise in person with the buyer, then tried to renege on that promise later. Lesson: It's part of your job to help your sellers to keep the big picture in mind, rather than allowing them to get hung up on something small.

Another example would be refusing to pay for a necessary repair (they will have to do it no matter what if they truly want to sell), or not paying for a one-year limited warranty, which may cost a few hundred dollars. Is it worth blowing a sale over something small?

Allowing Emotional Issues to Dictate the Transaction

As I mentioned above, a home sale is a business transaction, although it can often be difficult to make this distinction when sellers have so much of themselves invested in their home. I have had a number of occasions when my clients did not personally like the people buying their home, but I had to gently remind them that they would not have to deal with them long, and then they could move on with their lives.

Don't allow your sellers' emotions to prevent them from getting the home sold. If they don't like the buyers, it doesn't matter, if the terms are all agreeable. This is one reason that people hire real estate agents to assist with their needs. A (good) agent will serve as a buffer for any raw emotions which may come out during the sale.

Keep the big picture in mind and move forward.

Selling at the Wrong Time

Selling with bad timing can happen at least three different ways.

- Sellers do not yet know where they're going,
- The home goes on the market immediately before the sellers have to move, or
- It's the wrong time of year.

If the sellers have no idea where they're going to move, it's not a wonderful time to put the home on the market, unless they simply cannot afford the home anymore, or if they're in some type of imminent danger, or some other unusual exception.

The inevitable outcome of listing too soon is that you will receive an offer from someone who wants to move in right away, and the sellers will be forced to either reject the offer or find temporary housing, then move yet again when they find the right home.

If your clients are building a home with a specific timeline in mind, or if they're starting a new job and they have some time to prepare, don't wait until it's too late to get the home listed. You don't want to leave the home vacant and (even worse) have clients who end up with two house payments while you are trying to sell.

We have sometimes had clients who spent too much time getting their homes ready to sell and missed the biggest selling season in our market (though the market here in the Austin area has since become more year-round and less seasonal in nature). You'll need to understand your local market. Don't let clients spend an excessive amount of time preparing the home if there's a risk of missing the primary selling season in your area.

Not Giving Potential Buyers Access to the Home

This is a critical point: buyers don't always work around the sellers' ideal schedule. If it is a reasonable time of day (i.e. you are awake and most normal people also are), encourage your clients to let buyers look. Even if things are in disarray, let them look. Even if the buyer's agent doesn't give enough notice, *let them look*.

Although I always try to prepare for showings the day before they happen (or at least several hours ahead of time) and I train our agents to do so as well, there are times when a buyer will spot a sign and ask about a home that is not on the "to view" list. Sometimes, they end up buying this home. Keep that in mind with your listings and instruct your seller clients accordingly. If they choose to turn down a showing because it's on short notice, they could be turning away a potential buyer.

Another good point which warrants mentioning here is to tell the sellers to *get out of the house when buyers are looking*. Preferably, this means going for a walk or going to run errands, but at the very least, they should go outside and give the buyers some measure of privacy while they are looking around with their agent. This is a big decision, and buyers never feel at ease when sellers are in the home hovering around them. Advise sellers to let buyers look on their terms. If they are genuinely concerned about valuables, ask your clients to lock them up somewhere.

What Does "Value" Mean?

I've had some interesting and frustrating experiences with sellers in our market, especially at times when homes were not selling as quickly. Some clients just don't seem to "get it."

At any rate, it seems logical that if they are buying another home locally, they can get a lot of bang for the buck, right? Well, the quick answer is yes. However, the part that is always fun to explain is that *this principle affects their home as well.*

Here is a typical exchange with someone looking to both sell and buy when the market is softer or more balanced:

CLIENT: I guess there are lots of homes to choose from now, right?

ME: Yes, the inventory levels are high these days.

CLIENT: So, we should be able to get a good deal, huh?

ME: I hope so. It depends on the home you choose, how long it's been on the market, whether it's already been reduced, factors like that.

CLIENT: Well, we want to buy sometime soon, but we're not in a hurry either. We want to buy it right.

ME: Well, I feel sure that we can find the right place at the right price for your needs.

CLIENT: Now, with our home, we were thinking that it's worth about $400,000.

ME: Hmmm... (*thinking of walking out the door*) Well, based on the comparable properties here in your neighborhood, I think your home will probably sell for around $350,000 or thereabouts. Any higher than that, and it's unlikely to appraise, which means the buyer won't be able to get a loan. I must look at your home from this perspective to make sure things go smoothly. Keep in mind, as you mentioned before, that we will have a lot of competition out there.

CLIENT: Well, those homes don't have the yard (or kitchen or upgrades or surround sound system or pool or robot servants) that we have. Ours should bring more than that.

At this point, our appointment is at a crossroads. If they're halfway reasonable people, I can generally convince them that I am right and that it would be a waste of time to overprice their property. If they're not, we will quickly part ways so that I don't spend any more of my time, money, and effort on this. I've been down this road before, and it is draining for everyone involved

I guess it's simply human nature to assume your home will be unaffected by the market conditions, since yours is so darn special. Conversely, any home you are seeking to buy can be purchased for a song, because times are tough.

How does this make any sense? Well, it doesn't, which is the entire point of this lesson.

More often than is comfortable, we proud few in real estate are the ones who must present bad news and tell our clients things that are unpleasant.

Do your best to be empathetic but give them the truth about what to expect. This is true service.

"Bring All Offers" and "Price Firm" are Not Synonymous!

Part of learning any business is learning the lingo. There are tons of industry-specific terms in real estate, but there are also some phrases I have seen so many times that I can easily decode the hidden meaning behind them, such as:

- **"Needs TLC"** or **"Handyman Special"** — In a nutshell, this means that you need some extra money set aside (possibly a lot of it) if you want to buy this property. There will be a lot of repairs and/or renovations involved. It's not for the weak of heart.
- **"Cozy"** — More than likely, this just means "small."
- **"Won't last"** — More often than not, I see this phrase when the home has already been on the market a long time.

Speaking of which, I was once working with some clients looking to purchase their first home, and they were clearly excited. We looked at a lot of homes, then we found a home that seemed like a great fit for their needs. It was priced within their budget, and it was larger than some of the other places we had seen. For some odd reason, the home had been on the market for over *five hundred* days! The listing agent put in "Bring All Offers!" in the MLS remarks.

Let me pause for a second here.

Along with the examples I gave above, "bring all offers" is a phrase that typically means "we are ready to get this place sold, and things are highly negotiable."

Without divulging too many specifics, we wrote an offer that was aggressive without being offensive. The buyers asked me when we should expect a response. I told them that since it had been on the market so long, the sellers should have a pretty good idea of what they could do regarding the price, so we should hear something soon.

Nope. It took four days to get an initial response to our offer. On day three, the listing agent told me that she was working on a "very reasonable counter" for us.

So, what did this constitute?

The sellers actually raised their listing price by $6,000 in their counteroffer to cover most of the closing costs we had requested. The listing agent told me that there might be "a small bit of room" on that counter. We were still roughly $16,000 apart. I told her that we would probably just be looking for another home, and I later confirmed that with my clients. Back to square one.

- Lesson Number One: Do not put "Bring All Offers!" in the MLS unless you know that the price is flexible. If you know it's super-firm, you are simply wasting everyone's time, including your own.

- Lesson Number Two: Set the proper expectations with your clients. If the house has been on the market for many months and you still don't have an acceptable contract in place, errors have been made. Accept some measure of blame, and work on improving the price and/or condition if possible. Tell them the truth!

Chapter 5

General Advice for All Agents

There are some pieces of advice that will serve you well no matter who your clients are or what type of service you're providing. This chapter will assist you in residential or commercial sales, ranch sales, leasing, or any other area.

SETTING EXPECTATIONS WITH CLIENTS

The notion of setting expectations doesn't sound glamorous, and it honestly isn't, but it is necessary.

When you begin an agency relationship with a buyer or seller, it's important for them to know what to expect and how you work.

- **Scheduling**—Are you available early in the morning, or late at night? Neither? Both? It's good to be upfront with your clients about when they can reach you.

- **Form of Contact**—I am open to any form of communication, but you may prefer text, or phone, or you may want to keep everything in writing in your email inbox. Whatever the case, be sure to tell your clients the best way to reach you. I try to tailor things to each client's preferred mode of communication, and I recommend doing this as much as you can.

- **The Contract Process**—This is critically important to explain, particularly when it comes to inspections and repairs. Spending some time explaining how the process works and giving your client realistic expectations can save you a lot of headaches later. Please read the earlier chapters about working with buyers and sellers to better understand this.

If you do a good job of setting these expectations and responding with empathy to your clients, you're far more likely to avoid legal issues. I understand that real estate classes are full of examples of lawsuits and various scary liabilities, including many cases when agents meant no harm but still ended up in court, but this is far more rare than you may have been led to believe Hopefully, you have errors and omissions (E&O) insurance to help with honest mistakes you may make, but I do want to share some general advice about how to stay out of legal hot water.

How to Avoid Getting Sued—My Humble Opinion

> **Important Disclaimer: I am not an attorney, so I am not giving legal advice here, nor am I qualified to do so. This is just my opinion and nothing further.**

I thought I should get that out of the way first, because of our current litigious society. There is no guaranteed method to completely avoid getting sued, because people can choose to launch a lawsuit over pretty much anything.

In marketing, as you have probably heard many times, perception is reality. In real estate, this is certainly no different. I have always tried to view this career as a service business, rather than as a sales job. If you treat your real estate clients as potential sales rather than building relationships, you will struggle to build a successful business. It's important to take some extra time to show empathy.

Please allow me to explain.

When I am training new agents (and experienced agents, for that matter), I often reference a book that I read a few years ago called "Blink" by Malcolm Gladwell (he is also the author of "The Tipping Point"—I would highly recommend reading both if you have a chance). In "Blink," Gladwell explores the way that people make decisions, usually based on trivial things. I enjoy books that make me think and sometimes there is a point that sticks with me, as it did in this case.

One of the most interesting applications of this book to our business comes from his analysis of doctor–patient relationships, and whom people choose to sue when something goes wrong in malpractice cases. They found that patients almost never sue a doctor that took time to show that they cared about them. In fact, *the surgeons in one study who were never sued spent an average of only 3.3 minutes longer with their patients than their colleagues who were sued.* Also, patients would usually choose to go after the doctors they liked the least, as opposed to those who might have been at fault.

A quote from this section says, "When a patient has a bad medical result, the doctor has to take the time to explain what happened, and to answer the patient's questions. The doctors who don't take time for their patients are the ones who get sued."

The lesson for this in real estate is: *Take the time to show your clients that you care about them.*

With all of that in mind, I would like to give you an acronym which may come in handy if a client ever calls you with a concern which could result in a lawsuit. I was thinking about how to best handle difficult and delicate potential legal situations, and I realized that there are a few supportive actions that I always try to take.

The acronym is "CARE," although I am not sure if the letters are in priority order. Here are the individual elements:

1. Remain CALM
2. Be AVAILABLE
3. Be a RESOURCE
4. Show EMPATHY

- *Having a CALM demeanor will often defuse a problem before it reaches the point that it turns into legal action.* If there is something terribly wrong, or if you've made an egregious error, you may have consequences to deal with, but being pleasant and relaxed helps keep things professional and as smooth as possible. In fact, the ability to remain calm in the face of a problem is the hallmark of a great agent, no matter where in the process you are (negotiations, repairs, etc.)

- *Being AVAILABLE is self-explanatory, but it still warrants mentioning.* If you get a phone call from a client who says that their septic system is backing up into the house, or they may have mold issues from a long-standing leak, it is important to get back to them. One time, I accepted responsibility for not getting a septic system inspected, but because there was so much going on that I honestly forgot to help my buyers arrange for this. People always appreciate honesty. Always.

- *As a RESOURCE, you are often the first person that your past client will call or email if there is a problem with their property.* As such, you should be prepared to direct them accordingly. In some cases, this simply involves giving them information on their warranty or a qualified repair person. In other more extreme cases, it may mean counseling them to contact an attorney (not pleasant, but occasionally necessary). I have only had to do the latter a couple of times, but I was glad to help. My primary advice is not to avoid the problem, as that will make it worse for you, I promise. Go ahead and return the call, even if it seems scary. As Zig Ziglar used to say, "If you're going to have to swallow a frog, you don't want to have to look at that sucker too long!"

- *Demonstrating appropriate EMPATHY is critical if problems arise.* Sometimes, clients just want to use us as sounding boards for issues they're dealing with. Keeping that in mind, try to put yourself in their shoes for a few minutes as you are talking. If you can successfully imagine yourself in their situation, you will be more effective in assisting them. I am not recommending that you become a therapist (although I have had my share of those conversations as well), but I do think it's important for your clients to understand that you seriously care.

I hope this acronym I created doesn't feel forced, since these really are the primary elements involved. I also hope you found this helpful, and I hope that you can apply it in your business.

As of this writing, I have never been involved in a lawsuit or mediation, nor have any of the agents who work for me. Why? Because we try to show our clients that we care about their issues, rather than simply denying responsibility and becoming defensive at the first hint of a problem.

Sometimes, I have had to admit that I or one of our agents made a mistake. This is never easy, of course, but it's always the best course of action when we mess up, rather than shifting the blame or arguing, neither of which does anything to defuse the situation.

This is the essence of having integrity and part of succeeding in any business. Also, I can sleep at night because I don't have anything extra weighing on my mind. If you want to have long-term staying power and a stream of happy client referrals, show them that you care and accept responsibility when you mess up.

Do your clients know that you care about them? If so, you will have buyers and sellers beating a path to your door.

"Are You Already Working with an Agent?"

This is a question that you should get accustomed to asking when you meet a prospective client who expresses interest in buying or selling real estate. I know that real estate agency laws are covered in great depth in pre-licensing classes, but I'd like to give you some practical notes on this as well. Some of this will be encouraging, I hope, while some of it will serve as a caution and help you to draw a strong ethical line.

First, allow me to be perfectly clear: soliciting someone else's client is wrong and you can and should get in trouble if you do this knowingly. If a home is listed, you should not be discussing with the seller what you can do better, or what their agent did wrong. If you meet a buyer at an open house or elsewhere, and they tell you that they've already committed to another agent, you must respect that and leave them alone.

Having said that, I also recognize that there are times when things are more nebulous, and you can be more assertive to try to gain the business.

Just because someone has spoken to an agent, this does not necessarily mean that they have established an agency relationship. If another agent is sending them listings, this is not enough, either. However, if they have signed a buyer's representation agreement, they are now completely off-limits. If you continue to pursue them, you are violating agency rules, and you're at risk of having legal issues.

I have met potential clients who have expressed that they were "kinda talking to another Realtor" or said something like this:

"Well, we met with one guy and he showed us some houses."

When you hear this type of thing, I think it's okay to push a little harder to find out whether they have signed anything with the other agent, or whether they even want to work with him. Most often, when they refer to another agent in this way, the door is open for you to pursue them as clients. People who have firmly decided or committed to another agent will usually express this in a clear, direct way.

I have never intentionally overstepped the agency boundary, partly out of respect and partly because I had it happen to me a few times early in my career and it's an unbelievably bad feeling. Signed agreements keep this from happening and providing excellent service before you even get to the agreement will go a long way toward warding off other agents from your clients.

If you have any additional questions about the rules surrounding agency, as with some other portions of this book, I recommend speaking with your broker.

How to Guide Clients Through the Real Estate Maze

I've been in the real estate business for a long time, and I am still amazed by how many agents and brokers I meet who are either misinforming their clients or allowing them to set their own preconceived expectations. Clearly, we are the professionals, and it's our job to guide our clients through the maze of the transaction.

I promise you that you will encounter plenty of agents who will expect you to do your part and to handle their part of the work as well. Typically, when faced with this type of lazy agent, I end up doing this because:

- I genuinely care about my clients and I want to get the deal done if it is at all possible
- I want the eventual payday
- I care about providing a pleasant experience for everyone

- I refuse to let a bad agent interfere with the process

I once sold a ranch property to some clients relocating from Maui. They didn't even have a chance to see the property before they got it under contract, so I took lots of pictures and video and tried to be as upfront as possible about the condition of the home. I wanted to minimize the potential "surprise" effect, so that they wouldn't arrive and be disappointed or let down. This is one example of setting the correct expectation with a client.

Thankfully, these clients immediately fell in love with the place when they arrived, and the buyer told me that "I don't think you have ever had a client who was happier than I am right now." I would love to hear this all the time, because I know that I'm providing a service and it's a great feeling when I have a chance to help people achieve their dreams.

Here's another example:

During some negotiations on a contract when I was representing the buyer, we quickly reached an agreement on price, then were hung up on the details of a leaseback (the seller wanted to stay for a few days after the closing to finish moving and clean up). I received a proposed leaseback amendment from the listing agent with a suggested leaseback amount of $25/day. This was a ridiculous proposal, as my clients' actual carrying costs for those days after they became the new owners would be $113 daily.

The other agent told me that the amount I mentioned was just too high and that it was above the rental market. I had to explain that it didn't matter what the normal rental market would bear — this was an *actual* expense, and my clients would be losing over $80/day if they accepted it.

This is a situation where the other agent should have set the correct expectation, rather than allowing the client to bulldoze and set their own terms. Thankfully, we got the amount we had requested, after I was able to coach the listing agent a little bit.

I learned another lesson that day: As a buyer's agent, it was my responsibility to set this amount for the leaseback rather than allowing the listing agent to do so.

Years ago, I helped a single mom who was a nurse, looking for a home in north Austin. We made an offer on a home (which was reasonable under the circumstances—I don't allow "lowball" offers with my clients except in extreme situations which might warrant this), and when I heard back from the listing agent, she told me that she was surprised it wasn't a higher offer, and that they had just reduced the price recently. She was trying to get me to convince my buyer to come in at a higher price, yet she had zero leverage.

After we had spoken for a few minutes, this brief conversation transpired:

ME: (Agent), do you have people beating down the door to buy this house?

LISTING AGENT: No. No, I don't.

ME: Have you had any other offers?

LISTING AGENT: No, we haven't.

ME: Then could you please go ahead and talk to your client and get me a counteroffer and I will see what I can do?

We closed on the property about three weeks later.

As you can see, I had to coach the other agent (who was a broker and had been in the business a *lot* longer than I had) on how to present the offer properly. She didn't set the right tone with her clients, and it made it more difficult for her to do her job correctly.

So, do you want to be a "super-agent?"

My best advice is to learn as much as you can so that you become a true expert in this field.

Adding value to the process is how we justify our commission. How else can you hope to gain the confidence of your clients and associates?

If you are an experienced agent or broker, you really don't have excuses when it comes to expertise. If you want to make a good living in this business, you *must* position yourself as the one in charge of the details. Although you're not the one making the purchase or selling decision, your opinion should always matter, and it should have some weight in the process. Otherwise, you are merely a passive "order-taker," and not a real estate professional who is bringing critical knowledge and ability.

I know that there is a learning curve in any business, and real estate has one of the steepest. If you are not experienced, surround yourself with good people, including a knowledgeable, "hands-on" broker, a solid lender, a skilled escrow officer or attorney, etc. This makes learning a lot easier, and it makes your transition into a new industry smoother, too.

To be clear, the learning never stops in this industry, even after years of selling.

Some Unique Tips for Communicating with Clients

Once, I was working with some clients who were … challenging, to say the least. They seemed to distrust everyone involved in the process, and both husband and wife alluded to suing the other party in the transaction more than once. They also threatened several times to sue their own lender. They never pursued any legal action, thankfully, since they had no case of any kind.

Since they both had trust issues, I decided that one of the best things I could do was to use the "BCC" (blind carbon copy) feature on any emails I sent to the other parties involved, so that they could see all of my written communications for themselves. This assuaged their fears that nothing was happening when we hit some strange lender-related delays. You can also use group texts to accomplish the same thing.

One big lesson I have learned in my real estate career is to always be proactive about telling my clients what is happening. I don't even like the word "proactive" as much these days, since it seems a bit trite, but it's the best word here. This assertive behavior applies for both buyers and sellers alike. I am not perfect at this, of course, and whenever I forget or put off a call or email, my clients inevitably contact me about that specific issue.

Here are a few examples that would warrant an email or phone call from me to my selling clients:

- Home is loaded in the MLS (send a link after calling)

- Followed up with agents who have shown the house (BCC thing works here, too)
- Received feedback
- Any marketing efforts of any kind

For buyers, here's another brief list of activities that merit contacting them:

- No response yet to initial offer after a day or so
- Any responses to offer/counteroffer
- Contact with title company about their file
- Contact with lender for any reason

In the instances above, sometimes I will pick up the phone. Other times, there might be a good reason to put it in writing, which means I will either CC or BCC my clients.

When does it make sense to use the CC feature? Well, it's useful sometimes to show a builder or the other agent or a lender that you are involving your client in the communication, to put subtle pressure on them to respond.

Other times, you might use BCC just to "prove" to your client that you are attempting a contact on their behalf, such as for feedback on showings, etc.

No matter what, I can assure you that doing these things will directly demonstrate your value.

If I had one piece of advice to give to new agents, other than the most important rule about having integrity, it would be to make a sincere effort to communicate with your clients. The only way that I can teach this easily is to ask you to put yourself in their shoes. What information would you want to have available if you were buying or selling a home, particularly for the first time or in an unfamiliar market?

Dealing with Conflict During Transactions

Difficult people are a part of the challenge when it comes to real estate. Sometimes, I get comments from my own clients along these lines:

"I can't deal with this guy. He doesn't seem to want to sell this house. Maybe we should find something else."

At this point, an inexperienced agent might give up and move on to the next home. However, I have a couple of quick tips/phrases to help you salvage your transaction (and your commission):

If you're the listing agent, you could say, "I recognize that the buyers are being jerks, but they're also the first ones to bring an acceptable contract price for you."

If you're the buyers' agent, try this one: "When we wrote the offer initially, I know that you thought this was the right place for you. Don't let the seller's bad attitude change that."

These phrases often help to put things in perspective for your client, and it can "reset" things a little bit. Clearing the air is a valuable sales tool if used properly.

One of the things I have said for many years is the following: "I understand that you don't like the (buyer/seller) very much, and truthfully, I don't like the way they're acting, either. Just keep in mind that we only have to deal with this person for about three more weeks, then you won't have to talk to them again or deal with them. They won't be living in the house with you, I promise."

That phrase alone has saved many sales for me personally, and for our company in general. It shows that you are paying attention to the dynamics of the sale *and* it uses humor to defuse a potentially volatile situation.

The Only Thing that Stays Constant Is Change

A few years back, I was working with some older clients who wanted to upgrade and get something newer. Their neighborhood had changed, and not for the better, unfortunately. After a few outings with them to look at houses, I realized something interesting: working with buyers who have been out of the market for an extended period (in this case, over 30 years) is remarkably similar to working with first-time buyers.

The questions that I answered for them seemed rudimentary to me, but I would imagine that just about everything had changed since their last purchase. I'm guessing that the contracts were far shorter in 1970, since so many of the paragraphs resulted from various lawsuits over the years. In fact, every time I attend a closing, it seems like the stack of papers to sign gets a bit taller for this very reason:

"This affidavit states that the lender did not inspect the property for evidence of squatters. This one talks about the fact that the lender is not responsible if there is a nuclear waste dump or an ancient Indian burial ground under the home. This one says that if zombies attack and break holes into the roof or windows, your homeowner's insurance will not cover this." … and so on. (Okay, so that last one was a joke.)

When we discussed financing, it probably seemed to them like I was speaking another language entirely, so I tried to take things slow. I looked over the loan estimate provided by the lender they were working with, and it seemed a bit high to me, but they didn't realize this, nor did they have any basis for comparison.

HOA fees, negotiations, contingencies, and everything else in the process were completely new to my clients.

"What happens after the offer is made?"

"How long do they take to respond?"

"How much earnest money is needed?"

"What is an option period and how does that work?"

All these questions came up while we were writing up the offer. The comparison between new buyers and those who have become unfamiliar with the market over time is something to keep in mind when working with buyers who haven't been through the process for a long while.

Our job is to educate and facilitate when working with our clients. For good or ill, we are sometimes called upon to educate other agents, lenders, and even outside family members during the sales process, but we do it because we are professionals. We need to guide our clients through the various issues they will face, rather than assuming that this is something they already know.

I've learned that when dealing with older clients or with clients who have been "out of the game" for an extended period of time, you will do well to remember whom you are speaking to, lest you scare them off with real estate "jargon."

THE SECRET INGREDIENT IS EMPATHY

This is a story/lesson that I originally shared on my blog in 2007. The lesson here feels no less pertinent today.

The day this happened, we had waited until it was a bit late to do much that would be fun for the kids, so we ended up doing a lot of much-needed grocery shopping instead. We tried to make it a little bit fun by allowing the kids to each pick out a book or toy, and they loved that.

While we were at the grocery store, we managed to completely fill two carts. As we wheeled to the checkout, I was pleasantly surprised that a young man who was sacking groceries (he was about 19 or 20) came running to help us unload the carts onto the little conveyor belt. This had never happened to me before, but I sensed that it wasn't part of the usual training. He simply wanted to help.

I was unloading one of the carts, and he was handling the other one. We did this in silence for a few seconds, then he said, "How are you guys doing tonight?" with actual concern in his voice.

Did we look that demoralized? I don't think so. He was just genuinely interested in us as people.

I told the truth with an *extremely* abbreviated version of some personal events, including the recent deaths of a couple of loved ones. He said, "Man, that sounds really hard. I see people come in here all the time, and they look tired or sad. It seems to me that they just need someone to care a little about them."

How intriguing is that? I was prepared to ignore him until he opened his mouth.

So, I decided to ask him about his day, and he said that he was tired as well, with work, college, and money concerns. I asked him where he was going to school, and what he was studying. He told me that he was studying psychology.

"That's why I ask questions," he said. We talked for another minute or so, then I told my wife that I would be right back.

I went looking for the manager, whom I quickly located. I told her that I wanted to take a minute to tell her about one of her employees, whom I pointed out to her. I told her that he was quite friendly and engaging, and that he made me feel welcome, and that I thought he was a great kid. She was a little taken aback (I guess people don't take time to say *pleasant things* about employees often), but then grinned widely and thanked me. I went back to pay, and as we were leaving, I told the employee that I put in a good word for him with the manager. His face lit up and he extended his hand. "Thank you so much!" he exclaimed.

This was a brief encounter, but it left an impression on me. My wife suggested that I write about the following lesson I learned from that experience, and I hope you find it helpful.

When your clients come to you, they are sometimes run ragged by the events of the day or by various events in their lives.

Do you make time to connect with them? Do you show empathy for their concerns? If so, they will be impressed with you and with your care for them.

If your clients sense that you sincerely care about them, this will pay both immediate and long-term dividends. I know some agents who are "all business," meaning that they want to spend their client time discussing properties and financing options so that they keep things moving toward the end goal, which is the sale. While there is nothing inherently wrong with this mentality, I've always found that it's easier to get things done and to clear any hurdles if you've made a personal connection with your buyers or sellers throughout the process. This young man at the grocery store exemplified the right kind of attitude for real estate.

I have yet to meet a single client who doesn't appreciate the fact that I care about them. If you want to develop the kind of business that will cause people to beat a path to your doorstep, develop empathy.

Merriam-Webster defines "empathy" as follows:

> *The action of understanding, being aware of, being sensitive to, and vicariously experiencing the feelings, thoughts, and experience of another of either the past or present without having the feelings, thoughts, and experience fully communicated in an objectively explicit manner; also : the capacity for this*

We are not called to be mind-readers, but having empathy is close. Can this be taught? That is an excellent question, and the answer is yes. I remember that my son showed excellent empathic abilities by the time he was five or six years old.

Empathy is the hallmark of a successful professional agent, and it will do wonders for your business if you can effectively practice this with your clients. Just remember the impact of my brief encounter and strive to have your emotional radar working properly. I promise you this will help in your career.

DEALING WITH UNPROFESSIONAL ADVISERS

One of the bigger challenges you will face in your sales career is the unwelcome advice of your clients' family and friends. Navigating this can be tricky indeed. You want to keep things moving forward smoothly with your clients throughout the transaction. You certainly don't want to risk offending a well-meaning parent or friend of theirs, no matter how misguided their advice may seem, or how pushy they become with you.

Some examples:

You get your sellers to agree to a reasonable price, then their neighbor says, "Wow! That sounds low to me. Is your agent just trying to get the house sold quickly so they won't have to work very hard?" The seller calls to pepper you with questions, and there is suspicion in her voice.

Or maybe you've worked hard to negotiate on behalf of your buyer client, then his dad tells him that he's paying way too much.

"How can he possibly afford that house on his salary? He hasn't even paid off his student loans yet!"

This is the kind of thing that makes you so valuable to the transaction. You are going to "earn your money" here.

Depending on your level of experience, this next "law" may ring true, or it may serve as a lesson going forward:

Seems like the amount of influence that a problematic family member or friend holds over the transaction is directly proportional to how badly you need the commission.

In other words, if you need the sale badly, that's when a random "expert" who has captured your client's attention will step out of the shadows to offer advice on the situation.

Maybe they used to be an agent back in the 70's.

Maybe they just bought a home and they are wary of the bad things that some agents do.

Whatever the case, it can often be difficult to overcome these types of objections.

In basic sales training at many brokerages, they cover the rudimentary objections that we often face in the field. However, I've never seen this specific topic addressed. Frankly, it's easier to address on a case-by-case basis, but there are some broad rules to follow.

First, here are some other examples to ponder:

- What do you do if your client's mother tells him not to buy a house in a certain area of town, but you've already finished finalizing the paperwork and are set to close on a house in that exact place?
- What about the "For Sale by Owner" house across the street that just went up for $30,000 over market? It makes your listing seem underpriced by comparison.

These are two real-life experiences that I have had in my own sales career. In the first case, I simply told his mom that this specific area of town was the only place where her son could find a suitable home at the desired price. The buyer had obtained custody of his two small children, and he needed space for them.

In the case of the FSBO, since the comments came from someone who wasn't that close to the seller, I told him that the guy across the street was deluded, and that he would never get anything close to that price anytime soon. And yes, that was pretty much verbatim.

Harsh words? Sure. The truth? In my opinion, yes.

My general rule of thumb when dealing with well-meaning friends or family members is to politely yet firmly remind them that I do this every day, and that I'm their representative, and that as a Realtor I already have a fiduciary responsibility to place their needs ahead of my own, and I promise that I take that seriously.

I never have to apply much pressure. The truth works wonders. Perhaps you will have to spend more time than is normal to salvage the deal, but it's certainly better than starting from scratch or losing the client altogether.

Don't let your buyers or sellers be misdirected by those around them if you know you're right. You should be the expert when it comes to these matters. Some of that comes with experience, though you can accelerate this with your research and with solid advice from your broker.

"I Hate to Be the Bearer of Bad News, But ... "

Over the course of my career, I have been the bearer of tough news for my listing clients many times. I never relish the thought of sharing bad news with anyone, but I must admit that my skills in this area have improved dramatically with experience.

I have a few tips to share that might help you if you are faced with delivering undesirable news to your own clients.

Options:

- Just say it. Sometimes, it's best to just spit it out, then deal with the explanation. If you're at a listing appointment, and you know that the home is worth substantially less than they were hoping for, you don't have anything to gain by beating around the bush. Get it out on the table. In fact, it might just save you some time if they're unwilling to listen to the facts, because you can make a quicker exit.

- You might consider prefacing your statement with, "I fully realize that this is not what you were hoping to hear," or something similar. It may or may not soften the blow much, but at least you tried, right?

- If they question your valuation of their home, tell them that you are forced to look at things as an appraiser would. I have said things like, "I think your home shows well, and you have a ton of nice upgrades. I think we might be able to find a buyer that will pay the price you want, but I don't think it will appraise for a loan, and then you'll have a new set of issues to deal with."
- Another good quote (feel free to steal it from me): "You might get a different agent to agree to list the home for that price, but it won't change the market value at all. Don't ever choose an agent based exclusively on the price they agree to list your house for, because you'll waste time and you still won't get the price you were wanting."

I hope that this is helpful for you. I'm known among my past clients as someone who is direct and honest, without being harsh. There is a fine art to communicating effectively.

What You Can Control

As a Realtor, one of the most important things you can learn and understand is which things are within your control and which things simply are not.

Here's a list of items that you control before, during, and after a real estate transaction:

- Your integrity (including the things you do and say)
- How you choose to grieve the loss of a sale or client
- Your marketing (both for yourself and for specific properties)
- Your own attitude
- Advice you give

Now, here's a list of things outside of your control:

- How your clients behave
- Whether your clients remain loyal
- Appraisal values

- Loan approvals
- Title issues
- Inspection issues
- How the clients on the other side behave
- How other agents treat you or your clients (or their own clients)
- The personalities of each person involved in the sale
- Family members who want to be involved in the transaction
- The market in general (good or bad)
- Competition from other agents or listings
- The ethics of other agents
- Builders and any promises they make
- What your friends do when it comes to real estate
- Whether or not your advice will be taken
- What other people will say about you or think about you
- The ability of others to do their jobs correctly and to keep promises
- How (or whether) other agents were trained to do things
- Emotions of buyers or sellers

Neither of these are exhaustive lists, of course, but hopefully this is a clear representation of how complicated this business can be. I have made the mistake of assuming I had control over things many times, when the reality is that all of us are subject to many outside factors.

I recommend keeping this idea in mind to preserve your sanity. Most real estate transactions will proceed and close smoothly, but some are just a whole lot harder, and that is part of being in this industry.

Chapter 6

Working with Related Industries

There are so many ancillary industries that are connected to real estate. Learning to navigate these is critically important to being a successful Realtor. You will naturally develop relationships with trusted friends, enabling you to provide a higher level of service to your clients—which should be one of your primary goals. Our work relies heavily on an interconnected web of other people in disparate businesses.

You Can Do Everything Right and Still Not Get Paid

One harsh reality of real estate is the fact that you can perform all your tasks correctly and still collect zero money. Why is that? Real estate transactions have a lot of moving parts, and you can only control a small portion of the whole.

Here is a short list of things which could go wrong:

- Lenders who do not assess things thoroughly enough or correctly
- Inspections which reveal problems that cause buyers to walk away
- Appraisals which are lower than the contract sales price
- Bad communication from the other agent involved, or from their clients, or from your own clients, for that matter
- Buyer losing a job (or quitting!) before closing

- Family members convincing a buyer to cancel the contract
- Title work which reveals liens the seller has not disclosed to you and which they cannot pay

Please understand that this is not an exhaustive list. It's simply something to give you a bit of perspective. All of these are things I have genuinely experienced in my own career. It's important to keep in mind in our industry that there are no "sure things," and some deals fall apart through no fault of your own.

Not to be the bearer of bad news, but this part never changes, no matter how long you are in real estate. There will always be flaky people and strange situations and challenges that arise which can directly affect your income. The best solution is to work with enough clients on an ongoing basis each month/year that you can withstand the loss or delay of an occasional sale.

Who's on Your Team?

When speaking to my clients and to the agents who work for me, I have sometimes referred to the real estate business as a jigsaw puzzle in which many pieces need to fit into place for things to work out properly. I was mulling over this idea, and I realized that it is even more intricate than that.

When you start in this business, getting handed a new buyer to work with can feel overwhelmingly difficult. How do clients manage to generate so many questions that you can't answer? You passed the licensing exam. You've lived in the area for ten years. Shouldn't you be prepared for anything that comes your way already?

Maybe this stuff isn't as easy as you originally thought.

You will learn how to solve problems faster with each successive try, like practicing with a Rubik's Cube. But are you actually solving the entire puzzle by yourself?

Each transaction is only as good as its supporting cast of characters. As I mentioned in the previous section, "You Can Do Everything Right and Still Not Get Paid" sometimes you are not in complete control of your paycheck.

If you are working with a motivated and qualified buyer, and you identify the perfect home and get it under contract, you are still at the whim of the inspector, title company (or closing attorney), and the lender, not to mention any outside influences, such as loss of job, change of heart, and so on.

I won't lie—it sometimes feels painful to give control of the transaction to someone else.

The key to getting it done smoothly is to choose your team carefully. I would highly recommend having players with solid integrity on your team. Still, it's your job to educate your clients about what to expect throughout and do your best to maintain good communication. Otherwise, they may not understand why the deal didn't work out and you may end up taking the blame, even if someone else was clearly at fault.

Selecting the Right Supporting Cast

As a real estate agent, you should prepare yourself to be approached by people wanting to sell you … well, almost everything imaginable related to our business. You will get random calls about insurance, and email drip campaign systems, and transaction management tools, and website "solutions," and much, much more. Additionally, you will become instantly popular with a host of other related businesses, especially once you start selling homes.

Here are some folks you will begin to meet and hear from:

- Loan officers
- Title companies
- Escrow officers
- Insurance salespeople
- New home salespeople
- Inspectors

I'm not knocking them or complaining about any of this, of course. You are part of their target market, and they're trying to make a living, just like you. If you have a broker who has long-established relationships, he/she will recommend favorites in these related industries. Over time, you may stick with these recommendations, or you may develop separate relationships of your own with those you trust.

No matter how this plays out, it's important that you have companies and individuals to recommend to your clients, who will be looking to you as the expert. Bear this in mind, because the people whom you refer must be of the highest quality. Though they are not a direct reflection on you, the right lender or escrow officer can make you look good and make your job easier.

My advice is to work with people who are responsive and take their businesses seriously, and with whom you feel comfortable. Beyond that, you want someone who is trustworthy and who keeps promises. The next few sections give more detail on some of the more important relationships you will develop in the industry.

CHOOSING GOOD LOAN OFFICERS

Quick note: In this section, I will use the terms "loan officer" and "lender" interchangeably, which is common parlance in our industry.

Assuming you work with buyers (and most agents do), you need to establish good working relationships with some local loan officers that you trust. Please note that I did say "local."

A good lender is worth his/her weight in gold as a member of the team for your real estate business.

More than likely, you will be approached by lenders early in your career. This won't ever stop, I assure you. Good loan officers know that developing relationships with real estate agents and brokers is the best way to grow their business.

Here are a few important and desirable traits to look for in lenders:

- **Responsive**—Find someone who answers their phone, even at odd hours. You will find that any loan officer who tries to work "typical" hours (Monday through Friday, etc.) is not as helpful as one who is available on evenings and weekends. I try to be respectful of a lender's time, of course, but there have been occasions when getting key information or a well-timed pre-approval letter has made the difference for my buyer clients getting the home they wanted.

- **Honest**—You may notice a theme throughout this book. I always think it's best to be honest with my clients, and I expect the same from the people I work with. Considering that, it's extremely helpful to find someone you can trust when it comes to mortgages.

In order to be as productive as possible, you should always recommend that buyers get pre-qualified before you start actively looking. If you determine a potential buyer is not able to buy right away, it will save you countless hours of showing and discussing properties.

During an actual transaction, you need someone whom you trust handling the loan, for obvious reasons.

- **Knowledgeable**—This should be obvious, but I'll say it anyway: You want to refer your buyer clients to someone who actually knows what they're doing, and who can come up with a solution that best fits their needs. The value of this to your success cannot be overstated.

- **Creative**—Obtaining a mortgage is frequently complicated, so you need a lender who is a good "big picture" person. Sometimes, it's necessary to have a "Plan A, B, and C" for more difficult situations. By "creative," I don't mean finding someone who will cut corners or do anything unethical or illegal, of course. Instead, I mean finding a lender who is willing to explore all of the options and solutions for your clients, rather than giving up too quickly if the loan looks difficult on the surface. Finding a creative and thorough lender is something that's hard to appreciate when you first enter the industry, but it can affect the outcome on some sales.

- **Good Rates and Competitive Fees**—You will want to have a good general idea of how mortgage interest rates are doing at any given time, both so that you can present yourself as a well-informed Realtor and so you can gauge where to send your buyers to get the best deals. Rates are part of the equation, but you also need to ensure that your lender is not charging exorbitant fees. This requires some of your time and effort to learn as you gain experience.

- **Personality**—Find lenders who are compatible with your working style and schedule (related to "responsive" above) and whom you sincerely like, because you will spend a good deal of time talking to them during an average month. If they grate on you, or if they are not pleasant in some other way, move on. I recognize that this sounds blunt, but there's no reason to torture yourself working on a regular basis with someone you don't like. This happens. It's okay to find someone else.

I hope this is helpful as you seek to find the best loan officers for your clients and for yourself.

Recommending Inspectors

> **I would like to offer a preliminary caveat before you read this short section: No matter what I advise here, don't go against the advice of your broker. I'm not going to offer you anything that I think is incorrect, but your broker may disagree with my approach.**

Part of my job is to help my buyer clients get the house they really want at the best possible price. Additionally, part of my representation includes the team that I have assembled to help during the buying process. This includes the lender (see previous section), inspector, and the title/escrow company which will handle the closing.

In real estate classes, we are taught not to specifically recommend an inspector, but to give a list and let the client pick from that list, or get their own inspector, should they choose to do so. In my own career, however, I have been working with the same inspector for over a decade now. I recommend him for every buyer, though I do tell each of them that they are free to choose whomever they want, and some do choose someone else.

Frankly, my preferred inspector is so meticulous and thorough that it can make my job more challenging. I strongly prefer this, rather than having someone who is sloppy or misses crucial details. I feel confident that he will provide the best service for buyers.

When you're new, you will have to lean on others to find an inspector to recommend, such as your broker, other agents, or the same person who inspected your home. Over time, it's great to establish relationships with high-quality inspectors whom you can refer with confidence.

I promise you that it's better to have someone who blows your sale upfront by finding something troubling than to have an unhappy client later or, worse, a lawsuit in which you must testify. That's the reason that real estate classes teach you not to suggest anyone specific, because it could result in some measure of liability for you and your broker. As I have noted elsewhere in this book, I have not encountered any genuine legal threats or problems at all, thankfully, but I understand the caution.

Recommending Title and Escrow Services

In our local area, almost all residential transactions are closed at a title company, which handles the research to ensure that buyers are getting a clean title to the property. They also handle the actual closing and funding for the transaction, making sure that all loans are paid off and all fees are correct, etc. They're also the final stop with your sale, and they'll be the ones disbursing your commission to your brokerage (or directly to you, if your broker allows this).

Some of my favorite times are attending closings with my happy clients and getting paid, and I'm guessing you'll feel that way, too.

This section is not intended to fully educate you about what title companies do, but rather to give you some advice on how to select a company to use.

If you're in a small market, you may only have one or two options. In Austin, we have many to choose from.

To be frank, the average title company will be able to handle your transaction with no big hiccups, and they may not even be particularly memorable. In this way, title companies are a little like restaurants: you will remember the great ones and you'll be excited to bring them more business, but the bad ones will leave a bad taste in your mouth and you won't ever want to return.

I have followed my current title account representative even though she has moved twice to other companies so far, because she knows the business well, she has been supportive of our agents (teaching classes and encouraging them), and she has our back when problems arise. These are all admirable qualities. She also convinced my wife to get her real estate license, so I am thankful for that. It has enabled us to work together, which is enjoyable, and it's also been a great financial blessing.

As with choosing a lender to work with, some of the process of determining where to place your precious contracts will be trial and error early on, until you "click" with a good company or individual.

As a listing agent, you will have the opportunity to direct a good deal of business to your preferred title company. You can do this as a buyer's agent, too, but it may be more of an uphill battle if the other agent has a strong preference.

My primary suggestion is to find a company with competent, courteous, helpful people. This becomes easier to discern with experience.

The Importance of Appraisals

After you have a contract in place, if the buyer is not paying cash, their lender will order an appraisal to establish the value of the home. Since this is a separate expense for the buyer, it's best to wait to order this until after the inspection is complete and any necessary repairs have been negotiated, in order to ensure the buyer feels good about moving forward with the deal.

Once the appraisal has been scheduled, the appraiser will typically visit the house and take pictures and measurements of every room, then work up a report that details the market value based on recent comparable sales, with a series of adjustments based on size, age, upgrades, condition, lot size, etc.

Why does the bank need this? Well, mortgages are collateralized loans, meaning they are based on the value of the collateral, which is the house in this case. For that reason, they want to ensure that the value matches (or exceeds) the contract sales price.

As a buyer's agent, you probably won't have any contact with the appraiser, though it happens occasionally. Listing agents will normally get contacted in order to help the appraiser gain access to the house, especially for occupied homes. It's always good practice to be nice and responsive, and to give any necessary information that the appraiser requests. If the house has any distinctive features which would make it more valuable and are not obvious from your MLS listing, you can share those with him/her as well.

Hopefully, up to this point, you have done the work to make sure that the house is not overpriced. When the market prices are increasing and there's plenty of demand, you may have a little leeway to price it aggressively high. When things are less certain or when the market softens, you will find that appraisers are more cautious about values.

While I hope you never have to "fight" an appraisal, this happens, too. I remember one from years ago that came in at $325,000, when our contract sales price was $375,000. We all wanted to see the appraisal to understand where that value came from, since it seemed so far off base. It turns out that the appraiser had used strict guidelines (only using homes within one mile sold in the past 90 days) which would have worked in an average neighborhood, but which were ludicrous in an area where all of the houses had several acres of property.

This is exactly how bad it was: the guy used one sale to determine the value of our property, and it was 1,200 square feet smaller.

The lender appealed the appraisal, and they expanded the area and timeframe. The new value came in above the contract price. This time, he used six sales. I remember that my clients were understandably nervous because of the initial report, but I explained to them that their appraisal now had more comps than I could even remember seeing, since the norm is around 3–4. They bought the home, and they later bought the lot next door as well.

Always keep the appraisal in mind when selling a home. Even if you manage to convince a buyer to pay way above market value, the deal may later be in jeopardy because of the appraisal. Price accordingly.

Chapter 7

Negotiating

This is one of my favorite topics, and I'm happy that I've learned how to negotiate effectively, as this is a valuable skill in our industry. When you have developed your own skills in this area, you'll be able to use them in other areas of your life, too. I have negotiated better deals on auto repairs and other services, and I've even used my skills when parenting.

THERE IS A DIFFERENCE BETWEEN BLUFFING AND GOOD NEGOTIATING

I have listed and sold many, many homes which received multiple offers. On occasion, when this happens, I get the sense that at least one of the agents thinks I might be bluffing.

Invariably, these are the agents whose clients do not "win" the house.

They don't seem to hear me or believe me, even when I say things like this:

"Obviously, my client wants to get the best deal possible for their home, but I really do have several other offers."

Or

"I assure you that I don't bluff. I strive to be as honest and upfront as I can in situations like this."

I suppose most of us have been conditioned to be skeptical of multiple offers, or bidding wars. Additionally, our industry doesn't have a stellar reputation for integrity and honesty, so this is worth keeping in mind.

Many times, I have had buyers' agents simply stand their ground, as if that will help their clients. Unfortunately, that just removes them from active negotiations, basically surrendering the property to someone else. This is a prideful agent move which ultimately harms the client.

Here are a couple of examples from my own career:

I once had an agent tell me that she was expecting a full-price offer the next morning, but that her clients were willing to take my offer if we would increase it by $5,000 (which was still not full price). I told my clients to wait, and the sellers accepted our offer with no changes. This was such a blatant and obvious lie that it was easy to see through the "strategy."

Years ago, there was an agent in Austin who had developed a reputation for manufacturing fake additional offers whenever he received a legitimate offer on one of his listings. I was warned about this from my previous broker, and I was able to pass this along to my clients when we did the paperwork. True to form, the agent did not disappoint us — he was "expecting another offer, or maybe two others," even though it had been on the market for over 100 days. How convenient! As it turned out, my clients got the home at their desired price.

I have always believed that it is my job to get the best possible price for my clients, both buyers and sellers. Thankfully, I haven't had to bluff to do so. You don't need to either. Simply allow things to play out and maintain your integrity and your reputation.

NEGOTIATING 101—YOU CAN'T MANUFACTURE LEVERAGE

I had to spend a bit of time thinking about the subtitle of this chapter. I think this captures the essence of what I am about to cover here.

First, what is leverage?

Simply put, when it comes to negotiating, leverage is anything which gives you the upper hand. This could include some type of extra knowledge that you have gleaned about a property or about the clients on the "other side" of the transaction.

Here are a couple of real-life scenarios which can help to put this idea into perspective:

- A house has been listed for 300 days. The original list price was $725,000, then it was reduced six times, and it's currently priced at $610,000. It has clearly been vacant for months. As a buyer's agent, it's clear that you would have some leverage on negotiating this one.
- You have a listing which hits the market on Thursday evening, and by Friday afternoon you have had 14 showings, with five agents promising offers. With this leverage, there's a pretty good chance you can sell this place for more than the listing price. Going forward, your clients can also probably make it clear that they don't intend to do repairs. This is true leverage.

Keeping that in mind, here are some tips from over two decades of my own experience. These are by no means comprehensive lists, but they provide a pretty good start.

Let me begin by giving a few quick pieces of advice for listing agents:

- If you don't truly have a written offer in your hand, don't try to convince anyone that you do.
- Never act personally offended by any legitimate offers that are presented to you in writing for your listings. Don't mock at the buyer's agent or use phrases like "My client almost fainted" or "We were surprised at the offer." Instead, try this: "Thanks so much for the offer. I will see what I can do. I'll be back in touch soon." There's no need to set a bitter tone from the outset. Bear in mind that you may have to work with the other agent for weeks.
- If you list a home at a crazy-high price, be prepared to defend it and/or to explain to your client why every offer you receive seems to be a lowball.
- If you get an offer in the first week or so in a good market, push for the full asking price. You'll probably get it.

And now, for buyer's agents:

- If you are making an offer in the first week that a place is on the market, make it strong, unless the place is clearly overpriced based on your market research.
- If you have an option period or some other due diligence period

which allows the buyer to back out of the deal within a certain number of days (as we do in Texas), make sure you get the inspection done and all repairs negotiated during that time. You will lose your leverage after that.

- When your client has identified a house, and you are about to submit an offer, don't tell the listing agent that you have no other options. In fact, make sure your client has a second choice if possible. It gives you more true leverage if the seller ends up being unreasonable.

- Go ahead and mention your assumption that the deal will work out when you're sending your initial offer letter or email. You can say, "I look forward to working with you on this transaction" or "I hope we can work together toward a smooth closing" or something similar.

- Don't try to pull comparable sales to justify a ridiculously low offer from your client. This comes across as confrontational and sets the wrong tone. I have written a few lowball offers in my day, but they are usually presented without apology. There is probably a reason for the number we chose. If you want to say anything at all, just say something like, "I hope we can come to an agreement. Thanks!"

No matter which side you are working for:

- Try to remember that you are representing someone else and it's their money on the line.

- Try not to act too excited or tip your hand too early. As an example, rather than saying, "This is the one!" try something like, "They have a strong level of interest, but we're still talking."

- Never underestimate the power of simple friendliness and rapport—I will readily admit that, all things being equal, I would rather work with an agent who seems nice. Most agents feel the same way. It's common sense, I hope.

Commission Issues

> There's no doubt that discussing commission is one of the most controversial topics in real estate. Most of us work on a straight commission basis, so we are fiercely protective of our income (as we should be, frankly).
>
> As we all know, there is no such thing as a standard rate of commission, so I will do my best to make my remarks here as generic as possible in order to appeal to the widest possible audience. Bear in mind that everything I share here is my opinion only, so you can choose to accept or ignore my advice.

If you spend any reasonable amount of time selling real estate, you'll undergo a "commissionectomy" at some point. There are times when I find it makes sense to give a discount.

If a client asks for a reduced rate of commission (and some will, I assure you), it's a good idea to have a response in mind ahead of time. This may differ depending on the situation. There are no fixed rules on it. Some agents choose to give everyone a rebate. Others never do. There's really no reason to feel pressured by either side.

Here are some considerations, no matter what you decide.

Hopefully, you are bringing tangible value to the transaction with your knowledge and service. With buyers, your assistance should help them to get the best deal they can for the home they truly want. With sellers, you could bring more net proceeds to your client even after they have paid you. On one transaction of mine in which I sold a home in Georgetown for some clients, my value was clearly demonstrated:

I had met with the sellers and established a reasonable value for their home. Before we put it on the market or signed a listing agreement, they found a potential buyer who wanted the house. I would not have been involved in that sale at all. Thankfully for all of us, that buyer eventually chose not to pursue the house, so I listed it for them, at a price which was high enough to cover the initial value plus my commission. After a short time on the market, it garnered an acceptable offer. However, I was able to leverage that to get a separate cash offer well above the asking price. The net result is that my clients walked away with an extra $26,800.

These clients were incredibly happy to pay me my full commission.

The bottom line: When you know that your service and knowledge add value, you should not feel afraid to stand your ground and charge your normal rate.

On the flip side, here are some instances when giving concessions might make sense:

- When you are still new to the business and trying to get some sales under your belt
- For past clients
- For clients who are both buying and selling homes, with you handling all of the transactions
- To assist someone in need (pro bono)
- To solve a small but irreconcilable difference between buyer and seller (such as a repair that a buyer wants, but the seller refuses to do)
- To reward someone who has been a good source of referrals for you

Obviously, you can choose whether you want to grant any concession at all, or perhaps your broker has rules which outline this. I just wanted to provide a few words on this topic.

Chapter 8

Things That Go Broke in the Night: Real Estate Horror Stories

Let me share a few stories about some of the more difficult clients that I've had the displeasure of working with over the years. I want to share these with you because they led to some difficult but valuable lessons for me. Hopefully, I can help you to avoid some of the potholes I experienced.

In my second year in the business, it felt like I was inundated with difficult scenarios to handle. I was young and hungry, but my business partner and I were able to garner a few high-end listings just by sheer force of will (plus we had nice suits).

Our first good listing appointment was in the upscale Rollingwood area of west Austin. The clients liked our enthusiasm (which was palpable), and they listed with us instead of a good friend of theirs. Sounds good, right? Well, the "friend agent" proceeded to solicit the listing at every turn, and the clients would relay to us that she thought we weren't doing anything right. If this happened today, I would call the agent directly and confront her, but this was 1997, and I was still getting my feet wet in the business.

In retrospect, I guess I could have pushed my broker for more help, but I didn't. You might already have predicted the outcome—the other agent bent the clients' ears during our entire listing period, then later reduced it heavily and sold it for them.

I have since learned to set boundaries with other agents.

Lesson: Don't let other agents mess with your clients!

Another lesson: One of our first high-end sellers seemed excited to list with us, but he wanted to put the home about $20,000 higher than our recommended price (maybe he was excited because he found two rookies willing to list his overpriced house). We were hungry and trying to establish ourselves, so we took it with the promise that he would evaluate the price and reduce it as necessary.

He did eventually reduce it, but only when he relisted it … *with someone else.*

Lesson: Don't take listings that are overpriced ever, even if you think it will help you to break into a new area.

Usually, this strategy only results in months of headaches and some embarrassment as well when the neighbors see your sign starting to grow cobwebs. This home was in an area we were marketing heavily, and it hurt our reputation. We ran out of money trying to continue marketing ourselves there, and we didn't return.

Keep this one in mind for future reference.

One of our first opportunities to sell a $1 million home was with a couple looking in the prestigious Westlake area of Austin. They were utterly unfamiliar with the neighborhoods and he had suddenly come into a lot of money because of a well-placed investment, but we were able to find their dream home quickly.

The listing agent was *far* more experienced than us, and she was one of those people who says "pretty as a postcard" to describe various views or features of the home, if that gives you any sense of how she operated. If this is your style, I apologize. It was way too syrupy for my taste, but the buyers seemed to eat it up. In fact, they liked it so much that they bought the home directly from the listing agent, and they later sold it with her for double the price they paid.

The primary mistake we made was calling the buyer's medical office to try to speak with her about a property she expressed interest in seeing, and when her employee grilled my business partner suspiciously about nature of the call, he explained that we were already helping the buyer. Later, the buyer was incensed that we had divulged this information to her staff.

All told, we lost about $99,000 in potential commissions with this specific client by not controlling the overall situation better, and by divulging too much information to an uninvolved party. The buyer's rep agreement did us no good, since we were faced with suing one of the largest brokerages in town or suing our freshly rich client. Since we were not directly involved in the actual offer and subsequent negotiations, we were told we couldn't make a case for "procuring cause," (which determines who the commission) even though the buyers found the property from our hard work.

Lesson: Don't ever give unnecessary information about clients to anyone.

I once met a musician who was a drummer for a nationally known band—I won't mention the name here, because it just seems like bad form. Suffice it to say that it wasn't Ringo Starr. The drummer and his girlfriend looked around quite a bit with us, and we soon found the proper home for his needs. His business manager was supposed to get in touch to begin the offer process, but we didn't hear anything.

Later, the drummer's mother-in-law called to see if they could get into the home to measure a room for soundproofing, and I mentioned that I hadn't ever heard from the manager. She was shocked, because she thought we already had a contract in place. After piecing it together, we were convinced that his manager simply stole his money and quit. Nice.

Lesson: Make sure you verify funds on a cash deal before you begin spending time with the client.

My favorite bad client story is this one: I listed a lovely luxury home on acreage in the late 90's, but it was in a remote area. This was tricky for us, because we didn't have any decent comparable sales to set the right price. We began the marketing, and we got way more showings than I would have expected for that area of town. Many of these flew in to see the place from our national magazine advertising.

Despite this activity, it took a *long* time for this property to sell (over a year as I recall). The sellers were alcoholics (not exaggerating here—just speaking plainly), and he liked to call me in the evening, slurring and complaining. Keep in mind that I was still new to the business. One evening, he called and started to cuss at me and attempt to bully me.

This was probably a turning point in my career, because it was the first time that I had to confront a client bluntly. I told him that I had known him for several months, and that I thought he and I had become friends now. I told him that he needed to calm down and stop talking before he said something he might later regret, and to sober up and call me the next day when he could think straight. He immediately apologized and we ended the call. He was still sorry the next day and apologized again, and that was the last time that happened with him. Later, we sold the property and all was right with the world when we got a big commission check.

> **Lesson: Clients may be our "employers," but that doesn't give them license to abuse us verbally.**

In 2001, I had a massive ranch under contract for a buyer client, which would have resulted in a commission of over $200,000 for us. The buyer came from an ad I had run in a national magazine. He seemed legit and above-board initially. After he decided to pursue the property, he asked me how much earnest money he should put up. I told him anything less than $100,000 would not be taken seriously. He pulled out his personal checkbook and wrote that check, which cleared the bank after we had a contract in place. As I said, it seemed legitimate.

After months of work, the deal fizzled because the buyer was never able to produce the funds to close. The buyer came to town several times to visit the property. He paid many thousands of dollars for an inspection and an independent appraisal, even though he was planning to pay cash.

To this day, I don't know what happened, but I think he was attempting to launder money for a foreign national, based on some of the things he said about his clientele as a "high-profile" financial advisor.

During the six months of my life that I worked on that transaction, my oldest daughter was born and I lost both of my grandmothers. I couldn't even celebrate or grieve properly, as I was laser focused on making this deal work. Ultimately, I could not control the fact that my "buyer" was not an honest, honorable person. He even tried to pose as his own attorney in written communications when he was trying to get his money back.

This happened long enough ago that Internet research was trickier, and this guy did seem to check out, so we were fooled. Make sure you verify the source of funds as much as you reasonably can. I cannot recall what he provided as proof of his funds, but we did check on this. It's also possible that his accounts were frozen by the government. Good times.

> **Twofold lesson: Do not be blinded by the promise of a huge payday, and vet your clients whenever possible.**

I attended a closing for a buyer for one of our ranch listings north of Georgetown in the early 2000's. All the papers were signed and notarized, then the buyer never brought the money. It turned out that he had made some type of investment scheme arrangement, pooling money from a retired teacher (or possibly from multiple teachers) as the down payment, then stealing it. The last we heard, his assistant had been jailed. I hope he ended up getting caught, too.

> Lesson: Actually, this one would have been hard to avoid, because he did have the money in his bank account, but we didn't understand until later that he had stolen it from others, with no intention of buying anything.
>
> Sometimes you can do everything right, and still not get paid your due.

Once, I helped a set of buyers who were eager to buy a home in an upscale area of town. They had come to an open house we hosted, and we showed them a few properties. It was a dad, along with his older parents, and his kids. They decided on the right house for their needs, and just before they were about to put an offer on the home, the dad was sued for custody of the children, so they were unable to proceed at all. That home would be the equivalent of a $2 million home today.

The only lesson I can think of to apply to this scenario would be to advise staying in touch with the clients you lose over financial issues like this, because they will probably eventually purchase a home. I was too new and inexperienced to do this back then, so I have no idea what happened with them later.

> Lesson: Keep in touch with people you know, since their living arrangements can change on short notice.

We had a listing that was referred to us in my first year in real estate, which was a thrill in and of itself. It was a giant home with a pool in an older neighborhood in northeast Austin. It was a weird floorplan, so it took a while to find a buyer, but we did eventually get a contract. There were no other agents involved, because the buyer came directly to us by calling from the sign in the yard. The night before the closing, my business partner and I went to the house to check on things to make sure it was all okay, because the carpet had just been replaced.

Well, it wasn't.

We actually spent hours cleaning the house at night in our dress clothes, trying to ensure that it looked perfect. The next day, we attended the closing in west Austin. After we were seated with the buyer, it was revealed through the escrow officer that we could not close because the buyer had lost his job and never bothered to tell anyone. I had to go and tell my clients, the sellers, who were excitedly waiting in the lobby to finalize things. We did later sell the house, thankfully.

> **Lesson: This particular one was utterly unavoidable. To state it simply, some people are going to lie or conceal embarrassing events. Life sometimes comes in to take things from us unavoidably.**

One last story: I had a higher-end listing that we put on the market in 2005, and we had gotten a contract in place. The buyers asked if they could move in a week or so before the closing, because they had seven kids and they were staying at a local hotel which was costing an arm and a leg. Although we were all a bit skeptical and wary of letting them move in early, we decided to allow it, but I advised putting in a punitive amount for the "holdover" period. In other words, if they didn't close by August 31st, 2005, they would be paying $300/day. We thought this would be sufficiently motivational to get them out or get it closed.

We were wrong.

They paid this amount for a month and then continued to pay for about a *year*! Yes, they paid $9000/month for almost 12 months. They kept claiming that the Patriot Act held up their money crossing the Canadian border, or that there was some other weird banking issue. They would get behind for a month or two, then pay a lump sum of $27,000 to the seller. Despite the huge monthly cash flow, she finally got tired of dealing with the tenants and decided to evict them for non-payment. The sheriff's office had to forcibly evict them from the property.

This was the longest time I have ever had a home marked "pending," and it didn't even close with that buyer. We got the property cleaned up and repainted, then we hired a professional home stager to come in and work her magic. The home was under contract again quickly, and we closed two years after we had originally listed. The seller told me that I had really "earned my money" on this one, which was gratifying to hear.

> **Lesson: If you can avoid it, DO NOT let buyers move in before the closing occurs! I have never again allowed this on my listings.**

My point in writing this chapter? Well, I am hoping that it might be halfway encouraging for you to realize that:

- "Wow, Jason has had a bunch of terrible clients in the past, but he is still in business and he's even running his own brokerage now."
- "Wow, my clients are nothing like that. Maybe I can do this after all."
- There is something to be learned on every deal, even the bad ones.

Chapter 9

Other Assorted Bonus Advice

This last chapter is a catch-all for some stuff I wrote that didn't seem to fit elsewhere.

INDUSTRY MYTH—"REAL ESTATE AGENTS AND BROKERS ARE GREEDY"

It's a common notion that Realtors and brokers are greedy and self-interested. I disagree. Speaking for myself, I got into this business for several other reasons (yes, money was among them, too):

- I enjoy looking at houses of all kinds—even ugly and "unique" ones
- I like helping people, and I truly think of our business as a service
- I like/need flexibility and variety in my schedule in order to thrive
- I wanted to do something with a high enough earning potential that my wife could quit work and stay home with our kids, although we didn't even have kids when I started
- I enjoy the independence and freedom of being self-employed, and I ran another business for a short while before I jumped into real estate

At any rate, I know many hundreds of agents, and some of them are certainly in this business for the wrong reasons, but most of them just want to make a decent living. I did a bit of research, and the median income for a real estate agent in this country in 2019 was around $50,000. It's tough to make a case for greed. If you throw in expenses, this is not a particularly exciting number.

So, with that in mind, why would a greedy person choose real estate as a potential career? Perhaps they hear about "million-dollar producers" and they assume that means those agents make over $1 million annually? I have certainly interviewed some agents who assume that a six-figure income is the norm in the first year or two (keep in mind our prices in Austin as you read this—we aren't in Manhattan). Yes, this is possible to attain, but it isn't typical.

The reality is that most of us aren't greedy; we are mostly a group of decent, hardworking people who are trying to make a living in a challenging and highly competitive industry.

I would submit that most agents are not particularly greedy at all, but they are *competitive*, and since many remain in this business despite difficult months (and years), I feel that as a group we are *optimistic*. Many times, we are banking on potential income rather than tangible commission checks. I guess that doesn't make for great gossip among homeowners, though it is the truth.

I feel thankful and blessed to be in real estate, despite the hits that we have taken from the media, discount brokerages, reports of our "dishonesty," etc. My career enabled my wife to stay at home and homeschool our kids for many years, and I wouldn't have it any other way.

Are Real Estate Clients Brand Loyal or Agent Loyal?

I remember learning about marketing and advertising during several of my college courses, and brand loyalty is a concept straight from Marketing 101. If you are unfamiliar with the term, in retail sales this describes the fact that some buyers never waver from their decision about which detergent to buy, or which toothpaste. Some people consistently use the same brand for these purchases, so they are "brand loyal."

Years ago, I met with a dynamic guy who had been running his own carpet-cleaning business, and he was looking to get into real estate. This freshly licensed young man had been referred to me by a dear friend, and I was more than happy to give him a chance.

During our time together, he mentioned that he was meeting with several companies, which I consider to be normal these days. In the end, his decision was between our company and a "big name" brokerage which shall remain nameless for the purposes of this book.

I was offering an exceptional deal for this person, but he was convinced that going with the national name would help to ramp up his business faster. The other company has a fine reputation locally, but they were not offering anything at all that would assist a new licensee to increase his/her business. I had leads by the bucketful from our websites back then, and I was willing to train him one-on-one. Additionally, he would have zero out-of-pocket expenses other than the commission split. None of these amenities would exist at the other brokerage.

When he called to tell me of his decision to work elsewhere, I told him that I was impressed that he called, and I also (gently) expressed my frank disappointment.

While I could understand his logic, I did tell him that he was likely to regret not accepting the offer to work with us, since the other company wasn't offering to help him in any perceivable way. I also told him that I thought he would understand after he had been in business for 6–12 months. I left the door open just in case he changed his mind later. I never heard back from him, and he is no longer in real estate. I genuinely think he could have been a big success given the *right* opportunity.

On this note, I know that I can't speak for other markets around the country, but here in Austin, buyers and sellers typically don't care a whole lot about the company name. They are much more concerned with the service and/or exposure that you can provide as an agent. In that way, I would say that the vast majority of people here are "agent loyal," and are more concerned about the level of individual service that they receive rather than the company name on the sign or business card.

I realize that this is not the case across the board, and that there is a small percentage of prospects who want to work with a specific company. This has always been an interesting phenomenon to me, since all the individual offices are run by different people, and the service experience is far from consistent. Unlike McDonald's or Crest toothpaste, you don't know what you're getting just by choosing a specific real estate "brand."

I have only come across a small handful of clients who seemed to care about the name of my company. Most of my clients never even think to ask which company I work for until they are holding my card or watching me put a sign in their yard.

Handling Tough Situations Gracefully

Over the course of my real estate career, I have grown a thicker skin, so to speak. In some ways it has simply become easier to accept when things don't work out the way I had hoped. I once lost a $213,000 potential commission when my buyer was caught for money laundering and possible association with terrorist funding. After that happened, I told my business partners that any other deal I ever happened to lose would be easier to stomach. In retrospect, I can safely say that this has remained true.

A few years back, my business partner Frank lost a sale because the lady that he was working with had a sister who insisted on representing her, even though she had absolutely no knowledge of the Austin area and lived many hours away. The buyer felt bad about it, but she allowed her sister to help, and our work and time were lost.

Rather than bicker or make her feel bad, Frank told her that he understood, and that he was sorry that he wouldn't be able to finish the transaction with her. He was gracious, probably a lot more gracious than I would have been under the circumstances.

About a year later, he received a call from this same client.

She said that she had always felt terrible about what happened, and she needed to sell her house. Since Frank had worked so hard on her behalf and since he was so nice when her sister forced her way into the transaction, she chose to work with us to list and sell her home, which was worth about $550,000 (a little bit more than she paid for it). Considering that the average home price back then was just over $210,000, this was a great listing for us. The $16,500 paycheck helped to heal a lot of wounds.

When tough scenarios present themselves, and they will, including some that have the potential to make you angry, do your best to remain calm and kind.

When I first started in real estate, I often used to allow my emotions to enter the picture in situations like this. Rather than taking the polite, measured, calm response, I felt the need to get a jab or two in when I heard this type of bad news.

Now, I can't say that I *always* accept hard news gracefully, but I certainly do try. Most of the time it's simply not worth arguing.

Obviously, there are rude people, too, and they are perhaps the exception to my rule, because I might actually be relieved to see them go.

Occasionally, I will provide lots of information and assistance to someone who is looking to relocate, only to later hear back from them that they have chosen another agent.

My response:

"I'm sorry to hear about that. Thanks for taking the time to call/email me. Could you give me any pointers on what we could have done differently to earn your business?"

Generally, there is no good response to this, but I do want this information. I always end the conversation with something like, "Let us know if things don't work out. We will be here." I do sometimes hear back from them if the other agent drops the ball.

Being gracious in defeat has brought back many clients in my career.

> **Bonus Tip:** One important lesson that I learned the hard way many years ago is to immediately offer to pay a referral fee to the relocation company if the buyer says something along these lines:

"I may have to use the company Realtor since they are paying my closing costs, moving expenses, etc."

I now instruct the buyer to tell their HR person that we will pay the fee, which is generally 30–35% of the commission. I managed to get two large corporate relocation accounts this way, which eventually resulted in tens of millions of dollars of sales for us.

Play it cool. You may reap the rewards later.

Patience Pays Off

Once, I was showing a handful of places to a couple who were looking to buy their first home. This was our first meeting, and things were going smoothly, although the homes themselves were in less-than-desirable condition because of the price range and the fact that all of them were either short sales or foreclosures.

He turned to me as we were leaving the third house, and asked, "So, Jason, how long do you usually work with a client before giving up on them?"

I have had this question posed to me in the past, but usually it comes from folks who have been actively looking for weeks (or months). Coming from someone I met about an hour before, it struck me as funny. It was also surprising, though, and it made me think, "What are my standards for this, anyway?"

I responded, "Well, actually, a few years back, I had one client that looked at almost 100 homes before deciding on the right one." Then I gave them a brief synopsis of how/why that happened. I just re-assured them that I am very patient, and that it takes an awful lot for me to get irritated. I went on to explain that I don't ever rush anyone, and that I want to help buyers find the right place, even if it takes a bit longer sometimes. This pleased him. They bought a home quickly, as it turned out.

Buyers who ask questions like this are going to be more respectful of your time and appreciative of the service that you provide.

I have worked with (almost) every conceivable type of buyer during my career, including those that want to use my time and expertise with no intention of working with me, people who are just looking at homes for fun, and those who are just plain disloyal. It's always refreshing to have clients who genuinely care about me and my time.

It's a particularly good sign if a buyer or seller says, "You have spent enough time on this for today. You need to get home to your family." or "Thank you so much for your time today. I learned a lot. This was great!" or (still waiting on this one to happen) "Jason, we have decided to name our next child after you."

But seriously, clients who genuinely respect you and your service are a blessing indeed, especially when they're pre-approved.

Magic Words

Remember when you were a kid, and you learned about the "magic words"?

If not, allow me to remind you: "please" and "thank you" have long been powerful phrases when dealing with others. Most of us learn this when we're kids.

These two already seem obvious to you, more than likely. Here's another (somewhat less popular) statement that can help you to earn and retain lots of business:

"I'm sorry."

The humility contained within this simple phrase carries a lot of weight. It shows that you care about the other person enough to apologize for your actions. It also demonstrates that you are not afraid to take responsibility when you mess up.

A few years ago, I was looking forward to meeting with some new clients who were looking to relocate from Brooklyn. I managed to catch him on the phone quickly after receiving his initial email, then we had a few email exchanges. We were scheduled to meet and look at about 10 homes. They wanted to meet just after the new year on the day after my wedding anniversary. I promised to email him before we met, to let him know the details (time, place, etc.).

Instead, I completely dropped the ball and forgot.

On the evening of my anniversary, while I was out celebrating with my wife, it struck me that I had messed up. I wondered if they found another agent to show them around since I never confirmed anything. I then realized that they had sent me an email from seven hours earlier.

"Jason, please let me know where we are meeting tomorrow. Thanks!"

It was about 11:30pm, so I sent a humble email, apologizing for my mistake. I did explain about my week, and the fact that it was my wedding anniversary, but in the end, I took responsibility for making things more stressful for them.

We had a great afternoon of home viewing, and they even decided to accelerate their relocation plans. They eventually closed on a house here, and I served as their agent.

Don't be afraid to accept responsibility when you make a mistake. None of us are perfect, and I have found that people are much more willing to forgive and forget when I do this. That goes not just for small errors (which this was) but for larger ones, too.

"You Really Should Have Pushed Me Harder!"

One of our agents had a listing that she was unable to sell, and the seller of that home used the phrase in the title of this section when they opted to hire someone else.

I had never had a client tell me that I should have pushed them harder, so this came as a surprise to me. It illustrates an interesting point about real estate sales (and sales in general, for that matter).

There are times when it makes sense to push a client, most commonly when they are having trouble making the right decision. This is not an easy task, especially for newer agents, but it is a necessity if you want to make real estate your long-term career.

Many years ago, I helped some cash buyers from California to move to Austin. Their original budget was $300,000 or so, but the home they fell in love with was a little higher, at $325,000. Let me preface this story by saying that I honored their price range—they drove by the more expensive place and they had to see it.

When the time came to make a firm decision, the husband was hung up on the higher price. Here's the conversation that followed (and this is pretty much verbatim):

CLIENT: I don't know, Jason. It's more than we wanted to spend, and I don't even have a job there in Austin yet.

ME: I realize that, but you're buying this house with cash from your current home sale. You are going to have enough money to buy two new cars, also with cash. You just have to cover the taxes and insurance on this place. Frankly, you could get a job flipping burgers at McDonald's and handle that.

They bought the house.

Don't be afraid to "push back" when your clients are being foolish. It's your job to represent their interests to the best of your ability. Part of that involves pointing out when they are wrong.

Much of the pre-licensing education in our industry is focused heavily on the liabilities that we face as Realtors. I remember thinking that the classes should all be called "1,001 Ways to Avoid Being Sued." While this is accurate in our litigious society, agents are afraid to speak their mind, even when the client needs direction.

Give your client real help and real opinions. This doesn't mean that you must guarantee the appreciation of their investment, or tell half-truths, or overlook potential problems. You are the professional. You are the one who does this every day. They need your help.

Chapter 10

Conclusion

Real estate is a bit of an enigma: Our business is neither as easy as clients think, nor as difficult as agents think.

Allow me to explain: Overall, the perception of the public is that we real estate agents have it easy. Show a home or two, help with some paperwork, then coast into commission town. I'm oversimplifying things, of course, but I know that I'm not far off here.

I wish it were true that my job was that simple. It involves being patient and diplomatic even in the face of major adversity, often from your own colleagues.

Sometimes, clients aren't loyal.

Sometimes, lenders make mistakes that jeopardize sales.

Frankly, there are a lot of moving parts when it comes to real estate sales, and a lot of juggling must occur.

Having said that, real estate isn't rocket science, either. When agents are struggling (I've been there), it's easy to blame outside factors:

- "Well … the economy has tanked."
- "Banks have tightened guidelines, so no one can get a loan anymore."
- "The media won't quit talking about how bad things are."

Believe me, I've had the same thoughts myself at times, but the bottom line is this: In any given market on any given month, people are buying homes. They might be buying fewer homes than they were a few months ago, but there is business to be had everywhere.

If you're an agent, grab your share of the pie.

I've always found it interesting how different the perspective is from the outside versus the inside of our industry. In my own naive way, I think it's the opposite of how doctors are perceived by others ("Wow, being a brain surgeon has to be an exceptionally hard job") compared with their self-perception ("Brain surgery ain't hard.").Alright, in fairness, they probably don't say "ain't."

If you read this entire book, kudos to you. I hope you found it helpful. It has been a longtime goal of mine to be a published author, ever since I was a kid. I have some ideas for more books, so we'll see how that goes. For now, I want to thank you again for spending your time reading my thoughts.

As I said in the introduction, you can feel free to reach out to call or text me if I can ever be of any help at all in your real estate journey. I mean this. I wouldn't say it if I didn't.

If you're in another market outside of Austin/Central Texas, please keep me in mind if you have clients moving into or away from this area. I would love to help, and I would happily pay you a referral fee if you are licensed (Remember that chapter about asking for the business?).

If you are in my local area, and you want to chat about getting into real estate, or about switching brokerages, I am always open to speaking to agents about working with our company. I can assure you that my business partner and I are some of the most easygoing and knowledgeable broker/owners you could ever hope to meet, and our commission split is competitive and fair. You also get to draw from my knowledge if we work together. If that sounds appealing, call me sometime and let's meet.

My cell number again is (512) 796-7653.

May God bless you in your real estate career. My choice to get into this business is one of the best decisions I ever made.

Index

A

Agents
   Excuses Made by 137
   Intelligence of 14
   Not Doing Their Share of the Work 88
   Resistance from 90
   Unethical 114
Apologizing 133
Appraisals 110
Appraisers 110
Attorneys 34
Austin 7, 138

B

Bad News 97, 99
Bankrate.com 48
Base Price 48
Beginner Tips 16
Best and Final 70
Bidding Wars 113
Bluffing 113
Boundaries in Client Relationships 122
Bracketing 62
Breaking Bad News 99
Breaking Points in Pricing 63
Bring All Offers 81
Brokers 129
Buffini, Brian 19
Builders 47

Business
   Getting More 18, 22, 27, 87, 124
   Necessary Compromises in Commissions 117
   Not Losing on New Home Sales 46
   Obstacles to 103
Buyer Representation Agreements 37, 87
Buyers 33
   Choosy 51
   How to Show Homes to 39
   New Clients 35
   Of New Homes 46
   Pre-Screening 70
   Qualification of 34
   Tips for Working with 58
   Understanding Their Needs 38, 56
   Who Are Out of Touch with Market Trends 94

C

Career Advice
   Choosing Real Estate 12
Cleaning Advice for Sellers 67, 74
Cleaning Junk Out of Sold Homes 55, 125

Clients
    Advising 97
    Bad Advice They Are Given 97
    Care for to Avoid Bad Outcomes 87, 133
    Gaining without Taking Another Agent's Client 87
    Greedy Ones Who Want to Take Your Commission 117
    Lack of Understanding of Market 80
    Loyalty of 128
    Setting Expectations with 38, 83
    Staying in Contact with 124
Closing 45
    Costs 71
    Timing of 71
CMA 61
Commission
    Issues 117
    No Standard Rate of 117
    Not Counting on 123
    On New Homes 46
Communication 91, 124
    Preferences in 83, 92
Comparative Market Analysis (CMA) 61
Comparing the Value of Homes 61
Comps 61
Confidentiality 121
Conflict 93
Construction Timeline 49
Contact, Forms of 83
Contact Information 9
Contacts, Business 124
Contactually 20

Contract
    Process 83
Counteroffers 71
Cozy 81
CPA letter 34

D

Dallas 7
Deadlines on Offers 57
Dealbreakers 77
Decluttering 67
Design Center or Studio 48, 50
Discretion 121

E

Elevation 47
Emotions Affecting Real Estate Deals 78
Empathy 95
Enjoyment of Real Estate 11
Escrow Services 109
Excuses Agents Make 137

F

Feeling Uncomfortable Is Expected 24
Financing 70
Floorplans 49
Forms
    Builder Contracts 49
    Buyer Representation Agreement 37
For Sale by Owner 98
FSBO 99
Funds
    Verification of 34, 121

G

Getting a Real Estate Job 13
Getting Business 18
Getting Started 16, 24
Gladwell, Malcolm 84
Going the Extra Mile for Clients 55
Greed
    In the Real Estate Business 127
    Of Clients 117

H

Handyman Special 81
Hangups Affecting Real Estate Deals 78
Hiban, Pat 19
Highest and Best 70
Horror Stories 119
Hours, Flexible 13
How to Avoid Lawsuits 84
How to Avoid Major Problems Transferring Properties 126
How to Be Realistic about This Business 100
How to Break Bad News to Your Clients 99
How to Get Listings 64
How to Get Your Start in Real Estate 16
How to Identify Good Loan Officers 106
Humility 133

I

Indecision, Overcoming 52

Information about Brokerage Services Document 37
Inspection 44
    Finding Good Inspectors to Recommend 108
    Pre-Pour Foundation 50
    Pre-Sheetrock/Frame 50
Integrity 14, 70
    In Listing Descriptions 81
    In Negotiations 113
    Talking to Clients of Other Agents 87

L

Lawsuits, Avoiding 84
Leadership 134
Legal Issues 84, 87
Leverage 114
Listening 56
Listings
    Appointments for New 64
    Best Time For 78
    Honesty in 81
    Importance to Career Viability 61
    Luxury 69
    Mistakes with 75
    Overpriced 120
    Photos of 67
    Sellers Unwilling to Allow Looking 79
    Tips for Gaining 66
    When to Turn One Down 65
Loan Letter 35
Loan Officers 106
Lockboxes 68, 70
Lot premium 48

Lowball Offers 90, 115, 116
Lying about Having Multiple
    Offers 113

M

Marketing 19, 20, 27, 31, 69
    Aimed at Real Estate Agents
        105
    Focus of 30
Master-Planned Community 48
MLS 36, 61, 91
    Effectiveness of 69
Move-In Problems 126
Multiple Listing Service (MLS)
    36, 61, 91

N

National Association of Realtors (NAR) 69
Needs TLC 81
Negotiating 113
Neighborhood Specialist 30
Networking 31
New Homes 46
    Upgrades Cost 49
Nextdoor 31

O

Obstacles to Business 103
Offers 58
    Deadlines on 57
    Lowball 90, 115, 116
    Multiple 70
Option Period 115
Overpricing 76

P

Patience 132

Personality Conflicts 93
Photography 67
Politeness 133
Pool, Value of 62
Preferred Lender 50
Preparation
    For Buyer Clients 38
Prequalification 50
Pre-Screening Buyers 70
Price
    Breaking Points in 63
    Overpricing Listings 76, 115
Price Firm 81
Price Range 63, 76, 120
Properties
    Pricing of 120
    Searching for 36
    Showing 38
    Specialized 62, 69
    Value of 62

Q

Qualification 34
Questions to Ask First Time
    Buyers 35

R

Real Estate Photography 67
Realtor.com 36
Related Industries 103, 104, 106
Repairs 44, 59, 72
    Neglecting 76
Representation Agreement 37

S

Scheduling 83
Searches for Properties 36

Seasonal Effects on the Market 78
Self-Respect 122
Sellers 61
    Difficulties with 79
    Listening to 56
Setback 48
Smells in Houses 74
Social Media 18, 31
Southwestern University 7
Spec Home 47
Sphere of Influence 15, 17
Square Footage, Value of 62
Staging 77
Sticky Situations 54, 130
Stories from Experience 119
Surveys 68

T

Tipping Point 84
Title Companies 109
To be Built 47
Traits Good Agents Have 13
    Availability 86
    Calmness 85, 116
    Confidence 15
    Discernment 123
    Discretion 121
    Empathy 86
    Friendliness 14, 116
    Honesty 14
    Humility 133
    Intelligence 14
    Leadership 134
    Likeability 13
    Listening Skills 16
    Patience 132
    Realistic Expectations 100, 103, 124
    Responsiveness 86
    Self-Respect 122
    Sense of Humor 14
    Service Mentality 14
    Sphere of Influence 15
    Thick Skin 16
    Trustworthiness 14
    Work Ethic 15
Traits Good Inspectors Have 108
Traits Good Loan Officers Have 106
Traits Good Title and Escrow Services Have 109

U

Unavoidable Problems 125
Uncertainty 24, 125

V

Value of Homes 62, 79
Verification of Funds 34, 121

W

Walkthroughs 50, 53, 73
Warranty 71
When to Give Up Some of Your Commission to Make a Deal Work 118
When to Sell 78
Who to Work with, Buyers or Sellers 61
Wisdom 119
Won't last 81

Z

Zillow 36

www.ingramcontent.com/pod-product-compliance
Lightning Source LLC
Chambersburg PA
CBHW061327040426
42444CB00011B/2810